Macbeth
Shmoop Learning Guide

About this Learning Guide

Shmoop Will Make You a Better Lover*
*of Literature, History, Poetry, Life...

Our lively learning guides are written by experts and educators who want to show your brain a good time. Shmoop writers come primarily from Ph.D. programs at top universities, including Stanford, Harvard, and UC Berkeley.

Want more Shmoop? We cover literature, poetry, bestsellers, music, US history, civics, biographies (and the list keeps growing). Drop by our website to see the latest.

www.shmoop.com

©2010 Shmoop University, Inc. All Rights Reserved.
Talk to the Labradoodle... She's in Charge.

Macbeth
Shmoop Learning Guide

Table of Contents

Introduction 4
- In a Nutshell 4
- Why Should I Care? 5

Summary 5
- Book Summary 5
- Act I, Scene i 7
- Act I, Scene ii 8
- Act I, Scene iii 8
- Act I, Scene iv 10
- Act I, Scene v 10
- Act I, Scene vi 11
- Act I, Scene vii 11
- Act II, Scene i 12
- Act II, Scene ii 12
- Act II, Scene iii 13
- Act II, Scene iv 14
- Act III, Scene i 14
- Act III, Scene ii 15
- Act III, Scene iii 16
- Act III, Scene iv 16
- Act III, Scene v 17
- Act III, Scene vi 18
- Act IV, Scene i 18
- Act IV, Scene ii 19
- Act IV, Scene iii 20
- Act V, Scene i 21
- Act V, Scene ii 21
- Act V, Scene iii 22
- Act V, Scene iv 22
- Act V, Scene v 22
- Act V, Scene vi 23
- Act V, Scene vii 23
- Act V, Scene viii 23
- Act V, Scene ix 24
- Act V, Scene x 24
- Act V, Scene xi 24

Themes 25
- Theme of Fate and Free Will 25
- Questions About Fate and Free Will 25
- Chew on Fate and Free Will 25
- Theme of Ambition 26
- Questions About Ambition 26
- Chew on Ambition 26

Macbeth
Shmoop Learning Guide

Theme of Power	26
Questions About Power	27
Chew on Power	27
Theme of Versions of Reality	27
Questions About Versions of Reality	27
Chew on Versions of Reality	28
Theme of Gender	28
Questions About Gender	28
Chew on Gender	28
Theme of The Supernatural	28
Questions About The Supernatural	29
Chew on The Supernatural	29
Theme of Violence	29
Questions About Violence	29
Chew on Violence	30
Theme of Time	30
Questions About Time	30
Chew on Time	30
Quotes	31
Fate and Free Will Quotes	31
Ambition Quotes	35
Power Quotes	39
Versions of Reality Quotes	44
Gender Quotes	48
The Supernatural Quotes	54
Violence Quotes	60
Time Quotes	63
Plot Analysis	67
Classic Plot Analysis	67
Booker's Seven Basic Plots Analysis: Tragedy	69
Study Questions	70
Characters	71
All Characters	71
Macbeth Character Analysis	71
Macbeth Timeline and Summary	73
Lady Macbeth Character Analysis	75
Lady Macbeth Timeline and Summary	77
Duncan Character Analysis	79
Duncan Timeline and Summary	79
Malcolm Character Analysis	80
Malcolm Timeline and Summary	80
Banquo Character Analysis	81
Banquo Timeline and Summary	82
Macduff Character Analysis	83
Macduff Timeline and Summary	84
Weird Sisters (the Witches) Character Analysis	85
Character Roles	86

Macbeth
Shmoop Learning Guide

    Character Clues 88
Literary Devices 88
    Symbols, Imagery, Allegory 88
    Setting 92
    Genre 93
    Tone 94
    Writing Style 94
    What's Up With the Title? 96
    What's Up With the Ending? 96
Did You Know? 97
    Trivia 97
    Steaminess Rating 98
    Allusions and Cultural References 98
Best of the Web 98
    Movie or TV Productions 98
    Videos 99
    Images 100
    Documents 101

Macbeth
Shmoop Learning Guide

Introduction

In a Nutshell

Macbeth is a tragedy by William Shakespeare written around 1606. The only Shakespearean drama set in Scotland, *Macbeth* follows the story of a Scottish nobleman (Macbeth) who hears a prophecy that he will become king and is tempted to evil by the promise of power. *Macbeth* deals with the themes of evil in the individual and in the world more closely than any of Shakespeare's other works. Shakespeare draws on Holinshed's Chronicles as Macbeth's historical source, but he makes some adjustments to Holinshed's depiction of the real-life Macbeth. Holinshed's Macbeth was a soldier, and not much more; he was capable, and not too thoughtful or self-doubting. In Shakespeare's Macbeth, it is the internal tension and crumbling of Macbeth, entirely Shakespeare's inventions, that give the play such literary traction.

Macbeth is also unique among Shakespeare's plays for dealing so explicitly with material that was relevant to England's contemporary political situation. The play is thought to have been written in the later part of 1606, three years after James I, the first Stuart king, took up the crown of England. James I was the son of Mary, Queen of Scots (cousin to Elizabeth I) and this less-than-direct connection meant that James was eager to assert any legitimacy he could over his right to the English throne (even though he was a Scot).

Shakespeare's portrayal of Banquo as one of the play's few unsoiled characters (in Holinshed's *Chronicles*, Banquo helps Macbeth murder the King) is a nod to the Stuart political myth. King James traced his lineage to Banquo, who is thought to be the founder of the Stuart line. In Act I, scene iii, the witches predict that Banquo's heirs will rule Scotland and later, the witches conjure a vision of Banquo's descendants—a line of eight kings that culminates in a symbolic vision of King James, who was crowned King of Scotland and England (and also claimed to be king of France and Ireland).

Shakespeare, whose theater company (the Lord Chamberlain's Men) became the King's Men under James's rule, seems intent on flattering the King. Shakespeare also dramatizes one of the king's special interests: witchcraft. In *Macbeth* the three "weird sisters" feature centrally in the plot. They show Macbeth visions of the future and manipulate his murderous ambition in a play full of dark forces and black magic. Witchcraft was a hot topic in England at the time and James even published his own treatise on the subject in 1597, entitled Daemonologie. As James's court play-maker, Shakespeare would've known that inclusion of the dark arts would interest the King.

Beyond the abstract of evil, James was also the target of the Gunpowder Plot in 1605, where a group of rebel Catholics tried to blow up the King and Parliament (this is the historical version of Guy Fawkes, that guy in V for Vendetta). Macbeth's murder of King Duncan, then, would have struck a sensitive chord with the play's audience. There's also another allusion to the Gunpowder plot during the Porter's infamous comic routine in Act II, scene iii. The Porter refers to Catholic "equivocators," which is a reference to Jesuit Henry Garnet, a man who was tried and executed for his role in the Gunpowder Plot. Garnet wrote "Treatise on Equivocation," a

Macbeth
Shmoop Learning Guide

document that encouraged Catholics to speak ambiguously or, "equivocate" when they were being questioned by Protestant inquisitors (so they wouldn't be persecuted for their religious beliefs).

Why Should I Care?

Macbeth is a story about power struggles among the elite. What makes *Macbeth* great is its incredible insights into what the lure of power can do, and how blind it can make a person to moral reason and common sense. By studying men (and one woman) of great power, we get a glimpse into their minds. As it turns out, they're not as infallible as we sometimes think they are. They suffer the same feelings that all regular people suffer.

It isn't just power politics, but human emotion that Macbeth focuses on. These things still influence the world. For example, Angelina Jolie has the power inspire you to listen up about genocide or human rights. Macbeth is no less subject to sticky human emotions, especially as they apply to the realm of attraction – just check out Macbeth's interaction with his wife as she inspires, or shames, him to action. Lady Macbeth constantly references his manhood, which is tied to his emotional state, but also plays out in his physical courage. Many critics contend that the seat of Lady Macbeth's power is not only her sharp mind, but her sexual appeal. Just imagine Lady Macbeth as Angelina Jolie. She's giving the speech about how she'd dash out her child's brains while it suckled at her breast. You kind of see why Macbeth is so messed up, right?

Power is attractive, and you can't deal with Macbeth without getting into the individual psyche (mind) of a man. Macbeth is at first determined to not murder Duncan (the King), is convinced by his wife to kill the King, and then is so destroyed by the consequences that he seems to be numb when Lady Macbeth dies. Let's not beat around the bush – the man is whipped, but he's also just a man.

So read Macbeth. Once you crack the tough language, you'll get a glimpse into the raunchy, grotesque, beautiful human emotions that are timeless and universal.

Summary

Book Summary

On a dark and stormy night in Scotland, Macbeth, a noble army general, returns home after defending the Scottish King, Duncan, in battle. (Macbeth, by the way, was totally awesome on the battlefield – he's good at disemboweling his enemies and he's proved himself to be a loyal, standup guy.) Along the way, Macbeth and his good pal, Banquo, run into three bearded witches (a.k.a. the "weird sisters"), who speak in rhymes and prophesy that Macbeth will be named Thane of Cawdor and King of Scotland. There's good news for Banquo, too – he'll be father to a long line of future kings of Scotland, even though he won't get to be a king himself.

Suddenly, the witches vanish into the "foul" and murky air. Whoa, think Macbeth and Banquo.

Macbeth
Shmoop Learning Guide

Did that just happen or have we been nibbling on the "insane root"? (Banquo really does say "insane root.") The next thing we know, a guy named Ross shows up to say that, since the old Thane of Cawdor turned out to be a traitor and will soon have his head lopped off and displayed on a pike, Macbeth gets to take his place as Thane of Cawdor. OK. That takes care of the first prophesy. We wonder what will happen next…

Macbeth reveals to us that the witch's prophecy has made him think, briefly, about "murder" but he's disgusted with the idea and feels super guilty about his "horrible imaginings." He says he's willing to leave things to "chance" – if "chance" wants him to be king, then he doesn't have to lift a finger (against the current king) to make it happen.

But later, when King Duncan announces that his son Malcolm will be heir to the throne, Macbeth begins to think about murder once again. He writes a letter to his ambitious wife, Lady Macbeth, who immediately begins to scheme about how to kill Duncan. (The first thing she needs to do is berate Macbeth and make him believe that he's not a "man" if he doesn't kill Duncan.) The King just so happens to be scheduled to visit the Macbeth's at their castle so that seems like a good time to take him out. Later, Macbeth hesitates about murdering the King – after all, it's Macbeth's job to defend the guy, especially when he's a guest in Macbeth's home. But, Lady Macbeth isn't having *any* of his excuses. She tells Macbeth to stop being a wimp and to act like a "man." Besides, it'll be a piece of cake to drug the king's guards and then frame them for the murder.

That night at Macbeth's castle, Macbeth sees an imaginary floating dagger pointing him in the direction of the guestroom where the king's snoozing away. After he does the deed, Macbeth trips out a little bit – he hears strange voices and his wife has to tell him to snap out of it and calm down. (Lady Macbeth, by the way, says she would have killed the king herself but the guy looked too much like her father.)

When Macduff (yeah, we know, there are more "Macsomebodies" in this play than an episode of *Grey's Anatomy*) finds the king's dead body, Macbeth kills the guards and accuses them of murdering the king. (How convenient. Now nobody will ever hear their side of the story.) When King Duncan's kids, Donalbain and Malcolm, find out what's happened, they high tail it out of Scotland so they can't be murdered too. Macbeth, then, is named king and things are gravy…until Macbeth starts to worry about the witch's prophesy that Banquo's heirs will be kings. Macbeth's not about to let someone bump him off the throne so, he hires some hit-men to take care of Banquo and his son. Fleance, (Banquo's son) however, manages to escape after poor Banquo is murdered by Macbeth's henchman.

For Macbeth, things continue to go downhill, as when Banquo's ghost haunts him at the dinner table in front of a bunch of important guests. (That's never fun.) Macbeth then decides to pop in on the Weird sisters for another prophesy. The witches reveal the following: 1) Macbeth should watch his back when it comes to Macduff (the guy who discovered the king's dead body); 2) "None of woman born shall harm Macbeth," which our boy takes to mean "*nobody* shall harm Macbeth" since *everybody* has a mom; 3) Macbeth has nothing to worry about until Birnam Wood (a forest) moves to Dunsinane. The sisters also show how has Macbeth a vision of eight kings, confirming their earlier prophesy that Banquo's heirs will rule Scotland. Rats! Banquo's heirs just won't go away. Macbeth resolves to do whatever it takes to secure his power, starting

Macbeth
Shmoop Learning Guide

with killing off Macduff's family (since he can't get his hands on Macduff, who has run away to England).

By now, nobody likes Macbeth and they think he's a tyrant. They also suspect he's had a little something to do with the recent murders of Duncan and Banquo. Meanwhile, Macduff and Malcolm pay a visit to the English King, Edward the Confessor, who, unlike Macbeth, is an awesome guy and a great king. (Shakespeare's English audience totally dug this flattering portrayal of King Edward, by the way.) When Ross shows up in England with news that Macbeth has had Macduff's wife and kids murdered, Macduff and Malcolm get down to the serious business of plotting to overthrow Macbeth with the help of English soldiers, who will do their best to help save Scotland from the tyrannous Macbeth.

Meanwhile, Lady Macbeth isn't doing so hot. She sleepwalks, can't wash the imaginary blood from her hands, and degenerates until she finally croaks. Macbeth famously responds to news of his wife's apparent suicide by saying that it would have been better if she had died at a more convenient time, since he's a tad busy preparing for battle. He also goes on to say that life is "full of sound and fury, signifying nothing." (William Faulkner liked this line so much he used it for the title of one of his greatest works, *The Sound and the Fury*.)

Oh well, at least Macbeth is safe because the witches have said "none of woman born shall harm" him, right? Not so fast. Macduff and Malcolm have recently shown up with a big army that's looking to put Macbeth's head on a pike. Then, Malcolm orders the troops to cut the branches from the trees in Birnam Wood for camouflage. Remember what the weird sisters said about Birnam Wood moving to Dunsinane? You know where this is *headed*, right? Macduff corners Macbeth in the castle, calls him a "hell-hound," and tells Macbeth that he, Macduff, was "untimely ripped" from his mother's womb. So much for Macbeth not being killed by any man "of woman born." (Apparently, being delivered via cesarean section doesn't count as being "born" in this play.) Macbeth says something like "Oh, no!" (he doesn't have much to say at this point) just before Macduff slays him and carries his severed head to Malcolm, who will soon be crowned king.

Act I, Scene i

- Three witches (a.k.a. the "weird sisters") meet on a foggy heath (an open plain) in Scotland, amidst thunder and lightening. (It's all very dramatic and mysterious.)
- They discuss when they'll meet again, and decide to hook up "When the hurly-burly's done, when the battle's lost and won." The implication is that they've been up to something really naughty.
- Note: Even though the play's speech headings and stage directions refer to these three lovely ladies as "witches," the term "witch" only shows up once in the play. The sisters are, however, called "weird" six times, which seems significant because the term "weird" comes from the Old English term "wyrd," meaning "fate," aligning the three sisters with the three fates of classical mythology. (You know, the ones who controlled man's destiny.) In the opening scene, though, Shakespeare doesn't name them at all – they're referred to as "we three," which only adds to their mystery.
- They agree to get together again before sunset, and let the audience in on their plan to

Macbeth
Shmoop Learning Guide

- meet Macbeth. It seems whatever they've been plotting has included him, as this is the first mention of our title character.
- The witches then call out to Graymalkin and Paddock, who are the witches' "familiars," or spirits (usually animals like cats) that serve the witches.
- All three witches then repeat a chorus that sets the tone for the play: "Fair is foul and foul is fair," whereupon they set back to their supernatural business, hovering through the fog and filthy air.

Act I, Scene ii

- Duncan (the King of Scotland), his two sons (Malcolm and Donalbain), and Lennox (a Scottish nobleman) gather together with their attendants at a military camp in Scotland. (Check out this nifty map of major locations in the play.)
- King Duncan's forces have been busy fighting against the King of Norway and the traitor, Macdonwald.
- A wounded Captain arrives, fresh from the field, where he fought to help Duncan's son, Malcolm, escape capture. The group asks the bleeding man for more news from the battle.
- The Captain reports that the battle wasn't looking so good – Macdonwald's forces kept arriving from Ireland and the Western Isles – until brave Macbeth fought through the "swarm" of enemy soldiers and disemboweled the traitorous Macdonwald.
- There's some hemming and hawing about Macbeth's great courage in the face of seemingly impossible adversity and the Captain continues his story: after Macbeth spilled Macdonwald's guts all over the ground, the battle flared up again when the "Norwegian Lord" brought new men to the field, but even this didn't daunt Macbeth and Banquo, who just redoubled their efforts.
- Then the Captain announces he's feeling faint from all the blood he's lost so he needs to see a surgeon, ASAP.
- The Thane of Ross arrives and announces he's just come from Fife, where the Scottish traitor, the Thane of Cawdor, has been fighting against Scotland along side the King of Norway. It turns out that Macbeth kicked serious butt here too. Sweno, Norway's king, is not allowed to bury his men until he hands over ten thousand dollars to the Scots.
- Duncan then proclaims the traitorous Thane of Cawdor will be executed, and Macbeth, responsible for the victory, shall have his title.
- Ross is sent to announce the news to Macbeth.

Act I, Scene iii

- The three witches meet again on the heath and check in about what everyone's been up to. The usual witchy stuff: one was killing swine; another recently asked a sailor's wife for her chestnuts. The sailor's wife told the lady to scram so the witches are going to punish the stingy chestnut hoarder by stirring up a little trouble (a storm with some crazy winds) for her husband's ship, which is currently at sea.

Macbeth
Shmoop Learning Guide

- The weird sisters are also going to torment the poor guy by depriving him of sleep and by "drain[ing] him dry as hay," which means the sailor's going to have some serious gastro-intestinal problems and/or that he's going to be unable to father children. (In the 16th and 17th centuries, it was common for people to believe in the existence of witches. It was also pretty common for people to believe that witches were in the habit of doing things like whipping up nasty storms and causing male impotence.)
- History Snack: as we know, Shakespeare wrote *Macbeth* during the reign of King James I of England (a.k.a. King James VI of Scotland), who was *really* interested in witchcraft – he authorized the torture of witches in Scotland in 1591 and also wrote a book on the subject, *Daemonologie*, in 1603. What started King James's witch-hunting craze? Historians note that it began in 1589, when James's betrothed, Anne of Denmark, sailed to Scotland for the wedding ceremony, the ship encountered a major storm and was forced to take refuge in Norway. James ended up traveling to Oslo, where the wedding took place. On his voyage back to Scotland with his new bride, James's ship encountered another crazy storm, which was blamed on witches. Later, six Danish women confessed to causing the storms that upset James's wedding.
- Witch #1, of chestnutty fame, also has a pilot's thumb, a convenient rhyme for "Macbeth doth come," heralded by "a drum."
- Hearing Macbeth's approach, the witches dance around in a circle to "wind up" a "charm."
- Macbeth and Banquo show up, and Macbeth delivers his first line: "So foul and fair a day I have not seen." Hmm. Where have we heard that line before?
- Banquo notices the witches (they're kind of hard to miss) and speaks to them, noting they are unlike the earth's inhabitants, yet are on the earth.
- The witches put their fingers to their lips, which does not deter the perceptive Banquo from noticing their beards.
- Only when Macbeth tells them to speak do the witches call out. They hail Macbeth as Thane of Glamis, Thane of Cawdor, and future King.
- Macbeth doesn't respond immediately. Banquo, who apparently took over the narration for these five lines, mentions that Macbeth is "rapt," as if he's in a trance. (Get your highlighter out – this word comes up a lot in the play.)
- Banquo asks if the witches will look into his future too. The sisters cryptically say he will be lesser and greater than Macbeth, and not too happy, but happier than Macbeth. And they say he will be father to kings, though he will not be a king himself.
- Macbeth says he's already the Thane of Glamis but it's hard to imagine becoming Thane of Cawdor, especially because the current Thane of Cawdor is alive. He demands to know where the witches got their information
- The witches don't respond, but simply vanish into the foggy, filthy air.
- Banquo suggests that maybe they're tripping on some "insane root" but conversation quickly moves on to the big news about their own fates, as promised by the witches.
- Ross and Angus, two noblemen sent by Duncan (the King), break up the party.
- Ross passes on that the King is pleased with Macbeth's battle successes of the day, and announces that the King would like to see him, and also that Macbeth is the new Thane of Cawdor.
- Macbeth does some private ruminating. If the sisters' first prophesy that Macbeth will be named Thane of Cawdor can't be evil if it's turned out to be true. On the other hand, the witch's prophesy could be evil, especially since it's got Macbeth thinking about something naughty.

Macbeth
Shmoop Learning Guide

- This is where we get the first inkling that Macbeth might be down for a little tyrannicide (fancy word for killing a king). He says he's just had a really awful and disgusting thought about "murder." These "horrible imaginings" make his hair stand on end and his heart beat really fast – he's also feeling as though his mind has been divided.
- While Macbeth is deep in thought, Banquo comments to Ross and Angus that Macbeth seems "rapt," in a trancelike state.
- Macbeth concludes his dramatic musings and says that he's just going to leave things to "chance." If "chance" wants him to be king, then he doesn't have to lift a finger (against the current king) to make it happen.
- They hasten to the King, and Macbeth and Banquo agree to talk more about everything later.

Act I, Scene iv

- Duncan asks after whether the Thane of Cawdor has been done in. Cawdor is indeed dead. As he faced his death, he confessed as that he was a traitor (not so much a revelation) and repented.
- Macbeth, Banquo, Ross, and Angus then meet the King. The King is grateful; Macbeth and Banquo pledge their loyalty.
- The King announces that his son Malcolm will be named Prince of Cumberland, which is the last stop before being King of Scotland. They'll all celebrate the good news at Macbeth's place.
- Macbeth takes his leave of the group and has an aside, noting that now Malcolm is all that stands in the way of his kingship. Macbeth tells us he's thinking naughty thoughts again and hopes nobody can tell that he's got "black and deep desires."
- Macbeth heads home before the party – King Duncan and his peeps will meet him at Glamis Castle (a.k.a. Inverness).

Act I, Scene v

- Lady Macbeth receives a letter from Macbeth, calling her his "dearest partner of greatness," and telling her of the witches' prophecy.
- Lady Macbeth says she's worried her husband's not up for killing the current king in order to fulfill the witches' prophesy. Macbeth, she says, is "too full o'th' milk of human kindness" and isn't quite wicked enough to murder Duncan. (Looks like Lady Macbeth isn't going to leave anything to "chance.")
- Lady Macbeth says she's going to browbeat her husband into action.
- When a messenger enters and announces that King Duncan will stay the night at Inverness as a guest of the Macbeths, Lady Macbeth tells us it'll be King Duncan's last night on earth.
- Then Lady Macbeth delivers one of the most interesting and astonishing speeches ever. She calls on spirits to "unsex" her, "make thick [her] blood," and exchange her breast "milk

Macbeth
Shmoop Learning Guide

for gall." Translation: Lady Macbeth calls on murderous agents to stop her menstrual flow and change her breast milk for poison (undo all the physical features that make her a reproductive woman). Basically, she suggests that being a woman and a mother could prevent her from committing a violent deed.
- When her husband (the guy who's "too full o'th' milk of human kindness") enters the castle, Lady Macbeth tells him that King Duncan's spending the night but he won't be waking up the next morning.

Act I, Scene vi

- Duncan, his sons, Banquo, and a bevy of noblemen arrive at Glamis Castle (Inverness), complimenting the Lady Macbeth, their "honoured hostess," for her seeming hospitality.
- Lady Macbeth is pretty charming here – she says that the Macbeth's are grateful for the "honours" bestowed on Macbeth by the king and tells the men to make themselves at home.
- There's a whole lot of very formal "You're so gracious." "No *you're* the one who's so gracious" talk here before Lady Macbeth finally takes the king to see her husband.

Act I, Scene vii

- Somewhere in the castle Macbeth sits alone, contemplating the murder of King Duncan. Now, pay attention because this part is important.
- Macbeth says that if it were simply a matter of killing the king and then moving on without consequences, it wouldn't be a big issue. The problem with murder is what happens afterward – Macbeth would be damned to hell in the afterlife. Macbeth also muses that murdering Duncan in his own home would be a serious violation of hospitality. He's supposed to protect the king, not murder him. Plus, Duncan is a pretty good king (if not a bit "meek") and heaven is bound to frown upon murdering such a good fellow. Things likely wouldn't go Macbeth's way come judgment day. Probably not a good idea to commit murder. Macbeth realizes he has no justifiable cause to kill the king and he admits that he's merely ambitious.
- In the midst of his doubt, Lady Macbeth enters.
- Macbeth announces "we will proceed no further in this business," meaning the murder plot is off.
- Lady Macbeth gives him a tongue-lashing, questions his manhood, and lays out the plan to get Duncan's guards drunk and frame them with the murder. She insists that Macbeth keep his promise to kill the King. She claims she'd tear a nursing child from her breast and "dash" its "brains out" if she had promised to do it. Therefore, if Macbeth can't keep his vow, then he isn't a man.
- Macbeth commends her for her strength (enough for the both of them, it seems) and he finally resolves to go through with the murder.

Macbeth
Shmoop Learning Guide

Act II, Scene i

- Banquo and his son, Fleance, are at Macbeth's inner court at Glamis.
- Fleance notes it is after midnight, and his father gives him his sword and dagger. He says he cannot sleep because of some "cursed thoughts" have entered his mind.
- This doesn't bode well.
- Macbeth then enters with a servant, and Banquo notes that the new Thane of Cawdor (Macbeth) should be resting peacefully considering the good news he got today.
- Banquo says he dreamed last night of the witches, and Macbeth claims he hasn't been thinking about them (as perhaps he was too occupied with planning the murder of the King. But he doesn't say that part). Again, they promise to talk about it later.
- Banquo leaves, as does the servant.
- Macbeth, left alone, has a vision of a dagger that points him toward the room where Duncan sleeps. The dagger turns bloody and Macbeth says the bloody image is a natural result of his bloody thoughts. He notes that nature seems dead in the world (a fitting setting for his unnatural act).
- A bell rings, which is a signal from Lady Macbeth that it's time to rock and roll.

Act II, Scene ii

- Lady Macbeth is more determined than ever for the murder plan to proceed.
- She has drugged the King's guards and, hearing Macbeth, worries he may not have been able to go through with the act. She says she would've killed Duncan herself, if he hadn't looked so much like her father in his sleep. (Apparently, now she's all family values.)
- Macbeth enters with bloody hands.
- Macbeth says two people woke up while he was in the act. One cried, "Murder!" but they both went back to sleep after saying their prayers. Macbeth is disturbed that he couldn't say "Amen" when they said, "God bless us," as he could have used the blessing, given how he recently damned his soul by killing the King.
- Lady Macbeth employs the "If you don't think about, it will go away" theorem, but Macbeth is still clearly disturbed at having killed a sleeping old man for his own selfish gain. He also worried because he thinks he heard voices saying things like "Macbeth does murder sleep!"
- Lady Macbeth tries to get her husband to focus on the matter at hand, which is framing the King's attendants. He won't do it himself, so she takes the daggers from him, smears the attendants with Duncan's blood, and plants the weapons.
- As Macbeth philosophizes about his guilty hands, Lady Macbeth comes back, having done her part.
- She hears a knock at the door, and hurries Macbeth to bed so that 1) they don't look suspicious, and 2) they can do a little washing up before all the "Oh no! The king is dead" morning hullabaloo.
- Macbeth regrets killing Duncan – he says he wishes that all the knocking at the door would

Macbeth
Shmoop Learning Guide

"wake Duncan" from his eternal sleep.

Act II, Scene iii

- Now that Shakespeare's given us a murder and a lot of spooky crazy talk from Macbeth, it's now time for a brief, comedic interlude. There's a ton of knocking and the Porter (the guy who's supposed to answer the door) does a lot of joking around about what it would be like to be a porter of "hellgate." Apparently, a porter in hell would be a busy guy since there are so many evil and corrupt people in the world.
- The Porter says maybe there's an "equivocator" at the door.
- Note: An "equivocator" is a person who speaks ambiguously or doesn't tell the whole truth. This is likely an allusion to the treatise written by the Jesuit Henry Garnet, who encouraged Catholics to speak ambiguously or, "equivocate" when they were being questioned by Protestant inquisitors (so they wouldn't be persecuted for their religious beliefs). It's also significant that Henry Garnet was tried and executed for his role in the Gunpowder Plot of 1605, when a group of Catholics planned to blow up the King and Parliament (they stored kegs of gunpowder in a nearby building). The plot failed but it was a deeply disturbing and shocking event that resonates in this play, especially where we've just witnessed Macbeth returning from the room where he has murdered the sleeping king.
- Then the Porter says, no wait, this castle's way too cold to be hell but, gee, who could possibly be at the door at this hour.
- It's Macduff and Lennox at the door – the two noblemen have come to fetch the king.
- The Porter makes a bunch of jokes about how drinking an excessive amount of alcohol, (which he's been doing all night), makes a man frisky but it also detracts from his "performance" in the sack. It also turns his nose red, makes him have to urinate.
- Enter Macbeth, the picture of sleepy innocence while he makes small talk with Lennox and sends Macduff to wake Duncan.
- Lennox notes that some spooky things have been happening all night – he heard a bunch of screams, there was a little earthquake, and the fire in his chimney blew out.
- Macbeth says yeah, it's been a pretty "rough night."
- Macduff reenters, disheveled at finding the King murdered. He raises a fuss as he sends in Lennox and Macbeth to go look at the dead King.
- Lady Macbeth and then Banquo hear the news after waking up to the commotion. Macbeth, Lennox, and Ross come back after looking at the King's body.
- Macbeth takes the time to begin a way-too-eager eulogy about the King's great virtues.
- Malcolm and Donalbain, the King's sons, are the last to wake up and hear the news that their father has been murdered, to which Malcolm replies, "O, by whom?"
- Lennox says the drunken guards covered in the King's blood and holding their daggers are a good bet.
- Macbeth casually announces that he killed both of the guards in a fit of pious rage, out of his love for the King. No one thinks it's weird that the guards went to sleep with the bloody daggers in hand.
- Lady Macbeth, upon hearing that Macbeth has done this, needs to be escorted out (this was not part of her plan).

Macbeth
Shmoop Learning Guide

- Donalbain and Malcolm privately decide that they probably shouldn't stay in the house where their dad was killed. Good thinking. Malcolm will go to England and Donalbain to Ireland, making it more difficult to murder them both.
- The dead king's sons slip out, unnoticed.
- Meanwhile, everyone else agrees to get dressed and then talk about how they're going to respond to the King's death.

Act II, Scene iv

- Ross chats with a conveniently placed wise old man, who is disturbed by the night's strange events – both the King's murder and the weird things going on in nature.
- Ross says the heavens are clearly troubled by the unnatural act (a king's murder) that took place on earth. "Nature" has gone haywire as a result: Ross notes that even though it's the middle of the day, it's completely dark outside. The old man watched an owl murder a hawk and Ross notes that Duncan's horses broke free in a rage, to which the old man adds that the horses ate each other. Yep, says Ross, I saw the whole thing happen.
- Macduff, yet another Scottish nobleman, shows up. He says the dead guards "were bribed" to murder the king and that Malcolm and Donalbain look pretty suspicious, having left town so quickly and all.
- Macduff notes that Macbeth is on his way to Scone to be crowned King, and Duncan is being put in a freshly dug grave.
- Everyone goes their separate ways.

Act III, Scene i

- At Macbeth's new palace in Forres, Banquo, alone on stage, delivers a soliloquy (a speech that reveals his innermost thoughts to the audience), announces that Macbeth is totally suspect – it's likely he played dirty to get the crown. (Remember, Banquo was present when the witches' prophesized that Macbeth would be king. The witches also said that Banquo's descendents would be kings as well.)
- Short of being horrified by Macbeth's act, he takes some time to note that this must mean his part of the prophecy, regarding his royal seed, will also come true.
- Banquo pipes down when the newly crowned Macbeth, his lovely Queen, and a posse of noblemen enter the room. (Macbeth is looking rather cozy wearing his new crown and hanging out in his new digs.)
- Macbeth speaks very sweetly to Banquo, calling him his honored guest and requesting his presence at a fancy banquet to be held that night.
- Banquo plays it cool and ever so casually says that he's sorry, but he has other plans. Then Macbeth ever so casually asks what Banquo will be up to, and finds out that he'll be riding off somewhere before dinner.
- Having obtained the information he needs, Macbeth changes the subject to the fact that

Macbeth
Shmoop Learning Guide

- the "bloody" Malcolm and Donalbain are suspiciously missing, and respectively hiding out with new friends in Ireland and England. Plus, it seems that Duncan's sons are busy "not confessing" to Duncan's murder – instead, they're spreading nasty rumors about their father's death.
- Macbeth adds a little "by the way" as Banquo leaves, asking if his son, Fleance, will be riding along with him that evening. Fleance will indeed be going, and upon hearing this, Macbeth bids them farewell.
- Everyone except for Macbeth and some servants leave the room.
- Macbeth then has a servant call in the men he has waiting at the gate.
- Left to himself, Macbeth launches into a long speech about why it's necessary and good to kill his friend, Banquo. Macbeth fears Banquo's noble nature, wisdom, and valor. Plus, if the rest of the witches' prophecy comes true, Macbeth notes he will have sold his soul to the devil (by killing Duncan) for Banquo's kids to take his crown.
- He concludes his speech by inviting fate to wrestle with him, and says he won't give up until he's won or dead. (Gosh. It seems like it's getting a whole lot easier for Macbeth to think about murder, don't you think? It is interesting to compare Macbeth's attitude towards murder here to what he was thinking at the beginning of the play.)
- The two men at the gate are brought in, and we discover that Macbeth intends for them to murder Banquo and his son while on their ride. Macbeth gives speeches to the two murderers about how Banquo is their enemy and anything bad that has ever happened to them is surely Banquo's fault.
- Macbeth says that no turn-the-other-cheek Christianity is necessary here.
- The murderers respond by saying that they are only "men," and then Macbeth uses the technique he learned while being berated by his own wife: he claims they're not real men if they're not brave enough to murder a man for their own good. (Seriously. It sounds like he's channeling his wife here.)
- The henchmen point out that such speeches are lost on them, as their lives are pretty crappy anyway. They're fine with taking a chance on eternal damnation.
- Macbeth notes that Banquo is his enemy, too, and he'd do the kingly thing and just have him publicly killed, except that they have a lot of mutual friends, which might make things a little awkward.
- The murderers agree to kill Banquo, after which Macbeth throws in that they'll have to kill the boy Fleance, too. He'll let them know within the hour about where to find Banquo, but right now he has to go get ready for a dinner party.

Act III, Scene ii

- Lady Macbeth asks a servant if Banquo is already gone, and finding he has left, asks the servant to get Macbeth for a little chat.
- Macbeth comes along, and Lady Macbeth tells him to look more chipper and not dwell on dark thoughts, as "what's done is done." Macbeth points out they've merely scorched the snake, not killed it.
- Macbeth compares dead Duncan's death as a state preferable to his; at least Duncan doesn't have to worry about loose ends.

Macbeth
Shmoop Learning Guide

- Lady Macbeth would rather he not be a downer at the party, and says as much.
- Macbeth says she should say a lot of really nice things about Banquo, who will be otherwise engaged and not attending the dinner party. ("Otherwise engaged" = dead.)
- Lady Macbeth thinks this is a bad idea, but Macbeth points out that so long as Banquo and Fleance live, his mind is full of scorpions.
- Lady Macbeth states that everybody dies, which may be a warning to Macbeth to cool it, or may be a self-reassurance that everyone has to go sometime, so her husband might as well murder their friend and his young son.
- Macbeth again points out that something dreadful will be done, and in one of her less astute moments, Lady Macbeth asks what that naughty thing might possibly be.
- Macbeth dodges the question, saying it's better for her to "be innocent" and not know his plans until they're accomplished and she can applaud him for it. (Hmm. It seems like Lady Macbeth no longer gets any say in her husband's affairs.)
- Macbeth appeals to nature to let night's black agents do their thing, and then he exits with Lady Macbeth.

Act III, Scene iii

- At a park near the palace, the two murderers are joined by a third. Only a bit of light remains in the sky.
- Banquo and Fleance approach on horseback and dismount to walk the mile to the palace, as usual.
- Banquo and Fleance have a torch, which is convenient for the murderers to see them by.
- Banquo begins with a friendly "it looks like rain" conversation with the murderers, and then is promptly stabbed.
- While being stabbed, he denounces the treachery and encourages Fleance to run away and eventually take revenge. In the meantime, the torch has gone out, and Fleance takes advantage of the darkness to escape.
- Banquo squarely dead and Fleance on the run, the murderers head off to the dinner party to report the half of the job they've done.

Act III, Scene iv

- Meanwhile, back at the dinner party, Macbeth, Lady Macbeth, Ross, Lennox, other lords, and attendants are about to share the new King's celebratory meal. Macbeth makes a big show of welcoming everyone, as does Lady Macbeth.
- The first murderer enters as everyone is being seated. Macbeth darts off to see the first murderer, who informs him that they've slit Banquo's throat, but that Fleance has escaped.
- Macbeth laments the loss, as now Banquo is dead, but Macbeth's fear lives on in Banquo's son, heir and threat to Macbeth's newly won throne. He says Fleance is but yet a young snake, and time will surely make him grown venomous with revenge. In the

meantime, at least Banquo is dead. The murderer is sent off, and Lady Macbeth calls Macbeth back to the party.
- And now the fun begins: Banquo's ghost shows up. Because the ghost is silent, he gets to creep around quite a bit before anyone notices. While everyone is busy not noticing, Macbeth raises a toast and calls special attention to Banquo's absence as unkindness or mischance on Banquo's part. This is particularly hilarious given the presence of…Banquo's ghost.
- Again Macbeth is invited to sit, and in the spot they've reserved for him sits…Banquo's ghost. Naturally, Macbeth goes into a fit, and the lords all take notice, while Lady Macbeth excuses him for these "momentary" fits he has had since childhood. She urges them to keep eating, and then corners Macbeth, who is still hysterical.
- Lady Macbeth asks if Macbeth is a man, because he's not acting like one so much as he is acting like a sissy. Lady Macbeth dismisses the vision as a painting of his own fear. Meanwhile, Macbeth is discoursing with the ghost that only he sees, and it disappears.
- Macbeth notes it is unnatural for murdered men to not stay murdered. He is also still pretty wired. At Lady Macbeth's chiding, he apologizes to the group for his momentary fit and seems normal again until the ghost shows up once more. Again Macbeth calls out a toast to the missing Banquo (he's just asking for it now) and noting the ghost, screams out at him that if he appeared in any other form, Macbeth's nerves would not tremble.
- After some challenging along this line, it's pretty clear the party's over, and though Macbeth tries to recover, he scolds everyone else for seeming to be so calm in the face of such a horrible sight.
- Lady Macbeth tells the now very worried lords to leave immediately, and as they exit, Macbeth philosophizes that blood will have blood.
- Morning is now approaching, and Macbeth points out that Macduff never showed at the party. He lets out that he has had a spy in Macduff's house. He promises to go to the witches the next day, and announces that he's in so deep a river of blood, it would be as hard to go back as to cross.
- Lady Macbeth, wearied, insists he just lacks sleep. The scene concludes with Macbeth suggesting that his fears are just the effect of being young at the murdering/tyranny game. They go to bed, with more murder to follow.

Act III, Scene v

- The witches again meet at an open place, this time with Hecate, the goddess of witches, who lays into the weird sisters in a lengthy, rhyming speech that sounds a bit like a nursery rhyme. She is angry at them for meddling in the affairs of Macbeth without consulting her first, as she could've done a better job. Also, she points out, Macbeth isn't devoted to them, but to his own ends.
- Nevertheless, Hecate will take over the lead in the affair, and she charges them to all meet in the morning, when Macbeth will come to know his destiny, whatever that means. Hecate will create more illusions to add to his confusion, and instill in him a false hope that he might save the crown yet.
- Meanwhile, some spirits sing that Hecate should "come away" with them.

Macbeth
Shmoop Learning Guide

- Then there's a catchy witch song and dance and everyone exits after Hecate.
- FYI: Some literary critics believe that Shakespeare wasn't responsible for this episode. Act III, scene iv, according to some, is far too hokey to be Shakespeare's work so it must have been added to the play some time between the time the play was first written (1606) and its publication, in the first folio (1623), which was after Shakespeare's death (1616). A fellow playwright, Thomas Middleton, may have written the snazzy songs in this scene.

Act III, Scene vi

- The same night, elsewhere in Scotland, the nobleman Lennox discusses Scotland's plight with another lord. They find it curious that Duncan was murdered, that his run-away sons were blamed, that Banquo has now been murdered, that *his* run-away son (Fleance) is being blamed, and that everyone has a major case of déjà vu. Plus, the murders of Banquo and Duncan were too conveniently grieved by Macbeth, who had the most to gain from the deaths. They call Macbeth a "tyrant," and then note that Macduff has joined Malcolm in England.
- Malcolm and Macduff are doing a pretty good job of convincing the oh-so gracious and "pious" King Edward of England, along with some English noblemen, to help them in the fight against Macbeth, the tyrant.
- FYI: Shakespeare's giving England and King Edward the Confessor (1042-1066) some serious props here.
- The other noblemen pray that Malcolm and Macduff might be successful and restore some order to the kingdom, even though news of the planned rebellion has reached Macbeth and he is preparing for war. The noblemen tell us that Macbeth had sent a message for Macduff to join him, and Macduff's answer was a firm "no." The deck seems to be stacked against Macbeth, at this point.

Act IV, Scene i

- On a dark and stormy night, the three witches are hanging out in a cave roasting marshmallows and chanting spells around a boiling cauldron, into which they cast all sorts of nasty bits, from lizard's leg to the finger of a "birth-strangled babe." Hecate enters, announcing "something wicked this way comes." Not surprisingly, Macbeth promptly follows. (So does a Ray Bradbury novel and cinematic adaptation, but not for another few centuries.)
- Macbeth gives the witches some props for being able to control the weather and conjure crazy winds that batter churches, cause huge ocean waves to "swallow" ships, destroy crops, topple castles, and so on. (Hmm...this reminds us of Act I, scene iii, where the witches say they're going to punish a sailor's wife by whipping up a nasty little storm for her husband, who is at sea.)
- Macbeth says he has some more questions about his future and he wants some answers from the weird sisters, pronto.

Macbeth
Shmoop Learning Guide

- The witches add some more ingredients to the cauldron, and then apparitions begin to appear, each addressing Macbeth.
- First, an armed head warns him to beware of Macduff. Second, a bloody child promises, "None of woman born shall harm Macbeth." Macbeth welcomes this good news and, assuming Macduff was born the natural way, Macbeth thinks he has nothing to fear.
- Though he has no need to kill Macduff now, he pledges to do it anyway – you know, just in case.
- The third apparition is a child wearing a crown with a tree in his hand. The child promises that Macbeth won't be conquered until Birnam Wood marches to Dunsinane. This seems about as unlikely as Macduff not being born of a woman.
- Given all of this, Macbeth feels safe that he won't be conquered in the upcoming war. But again, to be on the safe side, he still asks if Banquo's children will ever rule the kingdom.
- He is warned to ask no more questions.
- He demands to be answered anyway.
- Macbeth is *not* pleased when he's shown a line of eight kings, the last of which holds a mirror that reflects on many more such kings. One of the kings in the mirror happens to be holding two orbs.
- Time for a History Snack: King James I of England (a.k.a. King James VI of Scotland) traced his lineage back to Banquo and, at his coronation ceremony in England (1603) James held two orbs (one representing England and one representing Scotland). Quite a coincidence, don't you think?
- The apparitions disappear and the witches tease Macbeth for looking horrible when he saw his future destruction. The witches do yet another song and dance routine and they vanish.
- Enter Lennox to find a perplexed Macbeth. Lennox tells Macbeth the news that Macduff has *definitely* run away to England, presumably to get some help for a rebellion.
- Get your highlighter out because this next bit is important: Macbeth says that from now on, he's going to act immediately on whatever thought enters his mind: "From this moment / The very firstlings of my heart shall be / The firstlings of my hand." In other words, no more thinking and contemplating about the pros and cons of being bad – he's just to do whatever the heck he feels like doing.
- Starting with… wiping out Macduff's entire family, especially his kids, since Macbeth doesn't ever want to see any little Macduffs running around.

Act IV, Scene ii

- At Fife, in Macduff's castle, Lady Macduff is lamenting to Ross that her husband has run away, which, even if he wasn't a traitor, makes him look like a traitor. Also, abandoning his family with no defense is pretty lame. Ross assures her that her husband has his reasons.
- Lady Macduff then has a funny bit of banter with her young son about how his father is dead. Before she can go to market to buy a new husband, a messenger enters advising her to flee with her children, as danger is fast approaching.
- Thinking she has done no wrong, she sees no reason to leave, though she notes in these times one need do no harm to come to harm. A murderer enters, claiming Macduff is a traitor. Macduff's son retorts, is stabbed, and then dies, leaving the murderers to pursue

Macbeth
Shmoop Learning Guide

his mother, Lady Macduff.

Act IV, Scene iii

- Near King Edward's palace in England, Malcolm and Macduff discuss what to do about Scotland's plight under the tyrannous Macbeth. Malcolm suggests finding a nice shady spot where they can cry their eyes out. Macduff says he's got a better idea – he suggests that they whip out our swords and fight like "men" against the good-for-nothing Macbeth.
- Malcolm says that's a good idea but he worries Macduff might have something to gain by turning on him, (Malcolm) and betraying him to Macbeth. Besides, Macduff doesn't seem like a loyal guy these days, having abandoned his family back in Scotland and all.
- Macduff says he's loyal and trustworthy.
- Still, Malcolm's a little paranoid so he decides to test Macduff by suggesting that even he, Malcolm, might make a poor king, were they to defeat Macbeth. Scotland would suffer, he says, under his own bad habits. Malcolm claims to have an impossible lust that would only get worse as he devoured all of the maidens of Scotland.
- Macduff at first insists there are plenty of maidens in Scotland, and Malcolm would be satisfied.
- Malcolm presses further about how bad he would be as king, and Macduff finally despairs that Scotland apparently is going to be in trouble either way.
- Malcolm then relents because he sees Macduff is truly devoted to Scotland, not to a political alliance. Malcolm then admits that not only is he not lustful, he's never even "known" a woman.
- Macduff and Malcolm are allied in the cause of taking Scotland back from Macbeth, and they have an army of ten thousand Englishmen at their backs, ready to fight and kill.
- Then a doctor shows up (rather unexpectedly) and talks about how King Edward is tending to a crew of poor souls afflicted by a nasty disease called "scrofula," which the King heals with his touch. It's implied that it's helpful to have a genuine king, as he gets his power from God and can do cool stuff like cure diseases and rule with an iron fist.
- We interrupt this program for a History Snack: Scrofula (what we now know is a form of tuberculosis that affects the lymph nodes and skin) was also called the "King's Evil" and it was thought to be cured by a little something called the "Royal Touch," a kind of laying on of hands ceremony that was performed by monarchs in France and England as far back as the middle ages. The healing ceremony was supposedly started in England by King Edward the Confessor (who's a swell king in *Macbeth*). In a book called *The Royal Touch*, historian Marc Bloch writes that King James I (who sat on the throne when *Macbeth* was first written and performed) wasn't exactly thrilled about performing this ceremony – he thought it was superstitious – but he did it anyway.
- Then Ross, a Scottish nobleman, appears in England and has a chat with Malcolm and Macduff about how Scotland is in a bad way. Macduff asks after his family, and Ross initially says they are unmolested by the tyrant Macbeth. He adds that if Macduff were to return, Scotland might gather and take up arms against Macbeth. Malcolm promises when they finally arrive in Scotland, ten thousand English soldiers will come, too.
- Ross then announces he has some bad news, actually. Macduff offers to guess at it, but

Macbeth
Shmoop Learning Guide

before he does Ross blurts out that, contrary to what he said before, Macduff's family has been gruesomely murdered.
- Macduff despairs and blames himself for leaving. Malcolm recommends that Macduff take his own advice and begin murdering out of revenge instead of crying. Macduff vows to slay Macbeth, committing to action instead of thought.

Act V, Scene i

- Back in Scotland, at Macbeth's castle in Dunsinane, a doctor waits with one of Lady Macbeth's gentlewomen. The two keep watch for Lady Macbeth's sleepwalking, which the gentlewoman reported began once Macbeth left to prepare the house for battle. The gentlewoman refuses to tell the doctor what else she's seen or heard during Lady Macbeth's nightly strolls.
- Lady Macbeth shows up walking (make that sleepwalking). She carries a candle, and the gentlewoman notes she insists on always having a light about her. They proceed to watch Lady Macbeth ramble through a tortured speech, at once trying to clean her hands of an imaginary spot (that would be blood, don't you think?) and chiding her invisible husband to be brave at what must be done. All the hand wringing and her question, "Who would have thought the old man to have so much blood in him?" leave little doubt as to what vexes the lady. (This is also where we get the famous line, "Out, damned spot!")
- In her sleep, she further assures her invisible husband that Banquo, being now dead, cannot trouble them. She goes back and forth in her speech between strength and self-pity – "what's done cannot be undone." The doctor diagnoses Lady Macbeth with a heavy heart and says he can do nothing to help her.
- Then the doctor says he's heard a lot of nasty little rumors that are floating around and says it sounds like Lady Macbeth probably needs help from the divine (a priest or God), not a doctor.

Act V, Scene ii

- Scottish noblemen, including Lennox, Menteth, Cathness and Angus converge in the country near Dunsinane, where Macbeth keeps his castle. We learn from Menteth that on their heels is the English army, led by Malcolm, his Uncle Siward, and Macduff. They'll all meet up near Birnam Wood. (Sound familiar?) We learn that Donalbain is not with his brother and that a great many young men have taken up arms with the English army.
- Cathness informs the group that the tyrant King is hell-bent on protecting Dunsinane, and though Macbeth is thought mad by some, and valiant by others, it's quickly becoming clear that his actions are in his own interests and not the nation's. Everyone agrees that Macbeth's a lousy king and needs to go. They all agree to fight wholeheartedly for Scotland.

Macbeth
Shmoop Learning Guide

Act V, Scene iii

- Macbeth is at his castle with the doctor and his attendants, and seems charged for battle. He is confidently bombastic – sure that he can't be defeated because of the sisters' new prophecy. He can't imagine Birnam Wood moving to march on Dunsinane, nor that any man could not be of-woman-born. Macbeth contends that with this knowledge, his heart is doubtless and fearless.
- Just then, a messenger enters with the doubtful and fearful news that there are ten thousand somethings marching to Dunsinane.
- Macbeth guesses that the somethings are geese. Seriously.
- The messenger says no, good try, but actually they're men coming to kill you.
- The messenger is much abused.
- Macbeth then thinks on himself. He says he has lived long enough; it is clear he will not have a peaceful old age, but rather will have fight to the last (which might be very soon).
- Macbeth confirms the news of the approaching army, as well as the lack of geese, via his servant Seyton, and then decides to don his armor to face them head on. He then asks the doctor about his Lady.
- The doctor reports she isn't sick so much as she is plagued by ill fantasies. Macbeth suggests that the doctor cure her, sooner rather than later.
- The doctor replies that the woman's got to fix herself.
- Macbeth attends to the battle again, and asks whether the doctor has the means to purge the English from the countryside of Scotland. The only sensible one in the lot, the doctor, says no amount of money could convince him to stay near the madhouse of Dunsinane.

Act V, Scene iv

- Malcolm, Siward, and Macduff meet with Menteth, Cathness and Angus, Lennox, and Ross at Birnam Wood. A plan is hatched to have soldiers cut down some branches to hide themselves under during the march to Dunsinane.
- Many of Macbeth's men have deserted him, and it's clear that those still siding with Macbeth don't believe in the cause. Still, Macbeth is so set in his certainty of victory that he is willing to let them march right up to Dunsinane, thinking the castle (and he) is protected from harm by the witches' prophecy. At this point, it might be wise to review that prophecy.

Act V, Scene v

- Macbeth (still at Dunsinane) insists that banners be hung outside the castle.
- Many of his former forces are now fighting against him on the English side, making it difficult for him to meet the army in a glorious blaze. He does not despair though, as Dunsinane is so fortified that he imagines the enemy army will die of hunger and sickness before he ever even needs to leave the castle. In other words, he's going to wait this one

Macbeth
Shmoop Learning Guide

out.
- In the meantime, a shrieking of women tells Macbeth that his wife is dead – it's suicide. Macbeth here launches into one of Shakespeare's (and literature's) best known and oft-quoted speeches, beginning "She should have died hereafter," meaning one of two things: she would've died eventually so she might as well have died today or, she should have died later because I'm super busy defending the castle right now. (As an aside, Macbeth's statement in this scene that "Life's but a walking shadow […] a tale told by an idiot full of sound and fury" is maybe the first occurrence of Existentialist thought in literature—it's also the basis of William Faulkner's famous work, *The Sound and the Fury*.)
- Macbeth is quickly distracted by the news that a "grove" of trees seem to be moving towards Dunsinane, which is all around bad news, since said "grove" is likely Birnam Wood. Macbeth, realizing the prophecy was as twisted as the prophets, decides to go out and face the army, leaving his fortress. He admits he is weary of the sun anyway, and if one must go down, best to go down fighting.

Act V, Scene vi

- Malcolm, Siward and Macduff land their army (covered with branches from Birnam Wood) outside Dunsinane. Siward will lead the battle with his son, and Malcolm and Macduff will take the rear and manage everything else.
- The soldiers drop their "leafy screens," the alarums sound, and the battle for Scotland begins.

Act V, Scene vii

- Macbeth appears on stage and compares himself to a bear in a bear-baiting contest (i.e. he's in a serious jam).
- History Snack: Bear-baiting is a blood sport that involves chaining a bear to a stake and setting a pack of dogs on it. Elizabethans thought this was great fun – bear-baiting arenas were located in the same neighborhoods as the theaters (just in case anyone wanted to take in a play and then top off their day of fun with a little animal cruelty).
- Then Young Siward enters – when he sees Macbeth, he demands to know his name. Macbeth's response? I'm "Macbeth" and you better be scared right now.
- They fight and Young Siward is slain.

Act V, Scene viii

- Macduff runs on stage looking for Macbeth (who is no longer on stage) and screams for the evil tyrant Macbeth to come out and show his ugly face.
- Macduff says he's hot to kill Macbeth with his own sword because he'll likely be haunted by his wife and kids if he doesn't. He begs "fortune" to let him find Macbeth so he can stab him in the guts.

Macbeth
Shmoop Learning Guide

Act V, Scene ix

- Malcolm and Siward (the father of the young man Macbeth recently killed) run across the stage looking for Macbeth. Siward says "This way, my lord" and then states some obvious facts for the audience – there's a lot of fighting going on at the castle, the thanes are fighting exceptionally well, and Malcolm's pretty close to victory.

Act V, Scene x

- Macbeth enters the stage alone and says he refuses to "play the Roman fool" (one who would choose noble suicide in the face of defeat – see *Antony and Cleopatra*). Instead, he will lash out at any living thing he sees, so valueless is life.
- Macduff enters and calls Macbeth a "hell-hound" and Macbeth talks a little trash in return: I already killed your family so you best be steppin' back now unless you want me to have *your* blood on my hands too.
- Macduff is having none of it. They fight, and Macbeth continues to be cocky. He says Macduff hasn't got a chance since he, Macbeth, can't be killed by anyone "of woman born."
- That's funny, says Macduff, because "Macduff was from his mother's womb / Untimely ripped." Note: That means he was delivered, prematurely, via cesarean section. And yes, Macduff actually refers to himself in the third person here.
- Upon hearing this news, Macbeth curses the "juggling fiends" who knowingly gave him a sense of false security by issuing a twisted prophesy.
- Realizing this, Macbeth says he will fight Macduff no more, yet he will not yield to Malcolm as an ordinary citizen.
- Then he thinks about it and realizes he really has to pick one. Though he knows he is beat by the prophecy, he fights to the last. Macbeth throws up his shield but is slain by Macduff anyway.

Act V, Scene xi

- Malcolm, Siward, Ross, the thanes and soldiers all assess what's been going down during the battle at the castle. It looks like Siward's son (Young Siward) and Macduff are missing.
- Ross delivers the news that Young Siward was slain by Macbeth. That's OK, says Young Siward's dad, at least he died "like a man." Old Siward goes on to say that if he had a lot of sons, he'd wish all of them could die in battle.
- Things get even better when Macduff shows up with Macbeth's severed head and says hey guys, look what I've got!
- Everyone turns to Malcolm and yells "Hail, King of Scotland." (Hmm. Isn't that how the witches greeted Macbeth back at the beginning of the play?)

Macbeth
Shmoop Learning Guide

- Malcolm hushes everyone and delivers the play's final speech, which goes something like this: All the Scottish thanes will be made earls, as in the English system, making them the first earls in Scottish history. Plus, everyone who had to flee the country because of Macbeth's tyranny can come back home now. But, all those who helped "the dead butcher and his fiend-like queen" are going to be in serious trouble. And, by the way, it turns out that Lady Macbeth killed herself. Don't worry, though, because King Malcolm's going to fix *everything* in due time. For now, it's time to party – everyone's invited to the coronation ceremony at Scone.

Themes

Theme of Fate and Free Will

Macbeth takes seriously the question of whether or not fate (destiny) or human will (choice) determines a man's future. Shakespeare seems, ultimately, to be interested in what it is that causes a seemingly decent man (Macbeth) to commit evil acts. On the one hand, the play is set in motion by the weird sisters' prophesy that Macbeth will be king, which turns out to be true. It also often seems that outside forces (related to the weird sisters, who are in many ways associated with the three fates) control Macbeth's actions. On the other hand, the play goes out of its way to dramatize how Macbeth deliberates before taking action, which suggests that he alone controls the outcome of his own future. Alternatively, some critics suggest that Macbeth's fate may be set in stone but his choices determine the specific circumstances by which he arrives at or fulfills his destiny. In the end, the play leaves the question unanswered.

Questions About Fate and Free Will

1. What is Macbeth's initial response to the weird sisters' prophesy? Does his attitude change at some point? If so, when does the change occur?
2. Macbeth is repeatedly described as giving the witches his "rapt" attention. Why is that? What does this suggest about Macbeth?
3. Do all of the witches' prophesies come true?
4. What role does Lady Macbeth play in her husband's actions? Is she always involved in Macbeth's decision making?

Chew on Fate and Free Will

Macbeth raises the question of whether free will or fate determines man's future but the play leaves the questioned unanswered, which suggests that, sometimes, human actions are completely ambiguous – we often never know why people behave the way they do.

In the play, Macbeth is fated to be king but he decides all on his own that he will murder Duncan in order to obtain the crown. This suggests that man's fate is predetermined but human will

Macbeth
Shmoop Learning Guide

ultimately determines how man will reach his destiny.

Theme of Ambition

Macbeth is often read as a cautionary tale about the kind of destruction ambition can cause. Macbeth is a man that at first seems content to defend his king and country against treason and rebellion and yet, his desire for power plays a major role in the way he commits the most heinous acts (with the help of his ambitious wife, of course). Once Macbeth has had a taste of power, he seems unable and unwilling to stop killing (men, women, and children alike) in order to secure his position on the throne. Selfishly, Macbeth puts his own desires before the good of his country until he is reduced to a mere shell of a human being. Of course, ambition isn't Macbeth's only problem. Be sure to read about the play's portrayal of "Fate and Free Will" also.

Questions About Ambition

1. What is it that compels Macbeth to murder Duncan? What drives him to continue committing heinous acts after the initial murder?
2. What does Lady Macbeth say about her husband's ambition? What does this reveal about her desires?
3. If Macbeth believed he was fated to have the crown, can he be credited (or blamed) with ambition in trying to gain it?
4. What fuels Malcolm's interest in defending Scotland? Do his actions up to the final battle indicate that he's prepared to be King? Is he guilty of or credited with ambition? What is the difference between him and Macbeth, if the office they hold will be the same?

Chew on Ambition

Ambition exists in both good and evil forms in Macbeth. On the one hand, some characters use ambition to act in the best interests of their country. On the other, some characters allow it to take the form of power-lust.

Macbeth portrays excessive ambition as unnatural and dangerous – it can ruin individuals and entire countries.

Theme of Power

Macbeth is interested in exploring the qualities that distinguish a good ruler from a tyrant (what Macbeth clearly becomes by the play's end). It also dramatizes the unnaturalness of regicide (killing a king) but walks a fine line by portraying the killing of King Macbeth. Although the play is set in 11th century Scotland (a time when kings were frequently murdered), *Macbeth* has a great deal of contemporary relevance. In 1603, King James VI of Scotland was crowned King James I of England, becoming England's first Stuart monarch. The play alludes to an unsuccessful Catholic plot (the Gunpowder Plot of 1605) to blow up Parliament and King James. Shakespeare also pays homage to the Stuart political myth by portraying Banquo as King James's noble ancestor.

Macbeth
Shmoop Learning Guide

Questions About Power

1. What kind of a ruler is King Duncan? How would you compare his leadership to that of Macbeth (once the latter is crowned king)?
2. What is the play's attitude toward the murder of King Duncan?
3. In Act iv, Scene iii, Malcolm pretends that he thinks he'll become a tyrant once he's crowned king. Why does he do this? What's Macduff's response? What's the overall purpose of this scene?
4. Does the play ever portray an ideal monarch? If your answer is yes, what textual evidence supports your claim? If your answer is no, why do you think the play never shows us a good king?

Chew on Power

In *Macbeth*, regicide (killing a king) is unnatural and evil but tyrannicide (killing a tyrant) is a perfectly acceptable action.

Although King Duncan is a good man and a virtuous king, he's also too "meek" to rule effectively. Macbeth, on the other hand, rules Scotland like a tyrant. The play, then, suggests that a truly good monarch should be a temperate ruler and strike a balance somewhere between Macbeth and Duncan.

Theme of Versions of Reality

"Fair is foul and foul is fair." That's what the witches chant in unison in the play's opening scene and the mantra echoes throughout the play. In *Macbeth*, appearances, like people, are frequently deceptive. What's more, many of the play's most resonant images are ones that may not actually exist. Macbeth's bloody "dagger of the mind," the questionable appearance of Banquo's ghost, and the blood that cannot be washed from Lady Macbeth's hands all blur the boundaries between what is real and what is imagined. This theme, of course, is closely related to the "Supernatural."

Questions About Versions of Reality

1. At the beginning of the play the witches say "Fair is foul, and foul is fair." What does this mean? Does this idea resonate throughout the play? If so, how?
2. How do Macbeth and Banquo respond to the witches' prophesy in act one, scene three? Does it seem real to them? Why or why not?
3. What kinds of hallucinations and visions occur in the play? What purpose do they serve?
4. Why is a doctor called in to tend to Lady Macbeth? What's wrong with her?

Macbeth
Shmoop Learning Guide

Chew on Versions of Reality

The witches' chant, "Fair is foul and foul is fair," echoes throughout the play – truth and reality are often murky in *Macbeth* and the distinction between what is "foul" and what is "fair" is frequently blurred.

Lady Macbeth's hallucination of blood stained hands suggests that no matter what she does, she can never wash away her guilt for the murder of Duncan.

Theme of Gender

Macbeth is notorious for its inversion of traditional gender roles – Lady Macbeth is the dominant partner (at the play's beginning) in her marriage and she frequently browbeats her husband for failing to act like a "man" when he waffles about killing the king. Lady Macbeth isn't the only emasculating figure in this play – the weird sisters cast a spell to literally "drain" a man as "dry as hay" and set out to ruin Macbeth. It's important to note that traditional gender roles are ultimately reestablished by the end of the play when Lady Macbeth is excluded from all decision making and goes mad before she finally commits suicide. The play is also notable for the way it portrays femininity as being synonymous with "kindness" and compassion while it associates masculinity with cruelty and violence. (A seeming paradox given that Lady Macbeth and the witches are quite cruel. The point seems to be, however, that these women are "unnaturally" masculine.) Macduff appears to be a lone voice in the play when he argues that the capacity to "feel" human emotion (love, loss, grief, etc.) is in fact what makes one a "man."

Questions About Gender

1. How does Lady Macbeth convince her husband to kill Duncan? What's her strategy?
2. What is meant when Lady Macbeth says Macbeth is too "full o'th'milk of human kindness"?
3. Why does Lady Macbeth call on spirits to "unsex" her? And, what does she mean by that?
4. How does the play define "manhood"? What is it that makes one a "man" in *Macbeth*?
5. How are women characters portrayed in *Macbeth*? What kinds of roles do they play?

Chew on Gender

For Lady Macbeth and her husband, masculinity is synonymous with cruelty and the willingness to murder.

In the play, women are portrayed as dangerous forces that can emasculate and ruin men.

Theme of The Supernatural

Witchcraft features prominently in *Macbeth*. The play opens, in fact, with the weird sisters conjuring on the Scottish heath. The witches are also the figures that set the play in motion when they accurately predict that Macbeth will be crowned king. Clearly, they have supernatural powers but their power over Macbeth is debatable. At times, the weird sisters seem to represent general anxieties about the unknown. They also seem to represent fears of powerful women

Macbeth
Shmoop Learning Guide

who invert traditional gender roles. Elsewhere, the witches appear rather harmless, despite their malevolent intentions. Ultimately, the weird sisters are ambiguous figures that raise more questions than can be answered.

Questions About The Supernatural

1. How do Banquo and Macbeth react when they first encounter the weird sisters in Act I, Scene iii?
2. The witches accurately predict Macbeth's future but do they control his fate? Why or why not?
3. How would you characterize the witches' speech? What does it suggest about their characters? How does it set them apart from other characters in the play?
4. Are there connections or similarities between the witches and any other characters in the play? If so, what are they, exactly?

Chew on The Supernatural

Although the weird sisters deliver a prophesy that sets the play into motion, they don't necessarily control Macbeth's actions.

In *Macbeth* the weird sisters represent the fear of the unknown.

Theme of Violence

Violence in *Macbeth* is central to action. The play begins with a battle against rebel forces in which Macbeth distinguishes himself as a valiant and loyal warrior. Later, Macbeth's murder of King Duncan is condemned as an unnatural deed but the play also raises the question of whether or not there's any real difference between killing a man in combat and murdering for self gain. Violence in all forms is frequently associated with masculinity – the play is full of characters (Macbeth, Macduff, Young Siward, and so on) that must prove their "manhood" by killing. Even Lady Macbeth asks to be "unsexed" so that she may be "filled with direst cruelty." At the same time, the play also suggests that unchecked violence may lead to a kind of emotional numbness that renders one inhuman.

Questions About Violence

1. The battlefield is central to most characters in the play, who have won their honors by killing others in this arena. Can the political realm of these players also be described as a battlefield? To what degree?
2. What kind of violence is acceptable on this political front?
3. Nature always seems to be rebelling against the unnatural acts going down in Dunsinane, yet violence is a central part of the natural world. Are humans any more than animals here?
4. The play ends with as much violence as the original battle against another traitor to the crown. Is there a suggestion here of cyclical and never-ending violence? Is there any way

Macbeth
Shmoop Learning Guide

to argue against Macbeth's claim that blood demands blood? And when will all the killing stop?
5. When Malcolm takes a break in England with Macduff, he wishes to stop and grieve. Macduff tells him instead that violence in the name of Scotland is a better cure. Yet when Macduff finds out his family is murdered, he grieves deeply and then turns to revenge. Is violence a justified reaction to a wrong, or is it just an emotion out of control that can be rightfully calmed with thought?

Chew on Violence

The reason that Macbeth's violence is inexcusable is because it doesn't play by the established rules. In *Macbeth*, organized violence is sport, and individual violence is uncivilized.

Throughout *Macbeth* violence and cruelty are associated with masculinity.

Theme of Time

Macbeth seems obsessed with the concept of time but it's often difficult to take away any definitive conclusions about the play's overall position on the theme. There are, however, several allusions to the idea that time literally comes to a halt when Macbeth murders King Duncan and takes the throne. Macduff's final remark that the "time is free" (now that Macbeth is defeated and Malcolm is set to take his rightful position as hereditary monarch) suggests a relationship between the seeming disruption in linear time and the disruption of lineal succession. The idea is that the country has no future without a rightful and competent ruler at the helm.

Questions About Time

1. What is the weird sisters' relationship to time? Are they the only figures capable of seeing into the future?
2. What happens to time when King Duncan is murdered?
3. What kind of future does Lady Macbeth imagine for herself and her husband?
4. How is Shakespeare's interest in representing the past (11th century Scottish history) in *Macbeth* relate the play's overall portrayal of time?

Chew on Time

Although Macbeth did everything in his power to secure his future on earth, by the end of the play, time has lost all meaning.

In *Macbeth* time comes to a complete halt and the "hours" are thrown out of joint when King Duncan is murdered. It is only when Macbeth is defeated that time is restored.

Macbeth
Shmoop Learning Guide

Quotes

Fate and Free Will Quotes

CAPTAIN
And Fortune, on his damned quarry smiling,
Show'd like a rebel's whore. But all's too weak;
For brave Macbeth -well he deserves that name-
Disdaining Fortune, with his brandish'd steel,
Which smoked with bloody execution, (1.2.1)

Thought: Here, the Captain describes how Macbeth overcame the rebel forces and defeated Macdonwald in battle. On the one hand, the Captain seems to suggest that Macbeth fought against and overcame "Fortune" with brute strength, "distain," and sheer determination. Yet, if we reread the first few lines of the passage carefully, we can also see that "Fortune," had already marked Macdonwald (Fortune's "damned quarry") for destruction. Fortune, it seems, smiled ("like a rebel's whore") on Macdonwald only temporarily, which implies that Macbeth was going to win this fight all along.

Note: Fortune (or Dame Fortuna, goddess of fortune and fate) is often portrayed as a fickle entity. With the spin of a wheel, Fortune can raise men up to great heights or cast them down at any moment. This particular passage is similar to an idea we see in *Hamlet*, where Prince Hamlet suggests that "fortune" is a "strumpet" who is responsible for the death of his father and his mother's hasty remarriage to a murderer (*Hamlet* 2.2.16).

First Witch
All hail, Macbeth! hail to thee, thane of Glamis!
Second Witch
All hail, Macbeth, hail to thee, thane of Cawdor!
Third Witch
All hail, Macbeth, thou shalt be king hereafter! (1.3.6)

Thought: The witches (who call themselves the "weird sisters" in this scene) confront Macbeth and Banquo on a heath and predict that Macbeth will become Thane of Cawdor and King of Scotland. (He's already the Thane of Glamis so the first greeting is more of an affirmation than a prediction.) The Third Witch also predicts that Banquo "shalt get kings," meaning, Banquo's heirs will one day rule (1.3.4). This, as we know, is what sets the action of the play in motion. We know that these predictions come true but the play asks us to consider whether or not these events are fated to happen.

In many ways, the weird sisters are associated with the three fates, which were thought to be able to control man's destiny. ("Weird" comes from the Old English "wyrd," which means "fate" and the witches are referred to as "weird" six times in the play.) On the other hand, this doesn't necessarily mean that the witches (or any other outside force for that matter) control Macbeth's

**Macbeth
Shmoop Learning Guide**

future. In the passages that follow, we see a lot of evidence that Macbeth's future is determined by his own will or, free choice. We'll want to keep all of this in mind as we read the play.

MACBETH
[Aside] Two truths are told,
As happy prologues to the swelling act
Of the imperial theme.--I thank you, gentlemen.
 Aside
Cannot be ill, cannot be good: if ill,
Why hath it given me earnest of success,
Commencing in a truth? I am thane of Cawdor:
If good, why do I yield to that suggestion
Whose horrid image doth unfix my hair
And make my seated heart knock at my ribs,
Against the use of nature? Present fears
Are less than horrible imaginings:
My thought, whose murder yet is but fantastical,
Shakes so my single state of man that function
Is smother'd in surmise, and nothing is
But what is not. (1.3.9)

Thought: After the witches vanish into thin air (having made their predictions), Ross enters and tells Macbeth that King Duncan has just named him Thane of Cawdor, which confirms one of the sisters' predictions. Upon hearing the news, Macbeth assumes the witches' prediction that he will become king will also come true and, here, he eagerly looks forward to his future (the "imperial theme").

But, then, Macbeth begins to deliberate about whether or not the prediction (a "supernatural soliciting" or, temptation), is a bad thing, especially since it seems to have stirred up "horrible imaginings" in Macbeth. At this point, it's clear that Macbeth's thoughts have turned to murdering King Duncan, who stands in the way of the prophesy coming true – as long as Duncan's king, Macbeth is not. What's so striking about this passage is not that Macbeth thinks about murder (he's a warrior and in the world of the play, murder and violence are going all around him) but, rather, that Macbeth is horrified by his own thoughts. His hair stands up on end, his heart "knocks" in his chest, and his mind is "shaken." In other words, Macbeth *knows* that the idea of murdering the King (the very man Macbeth has just defended in battle) is wicked. By the way, the witches *never* say anything to Macbeth about murdering Duncan in order to make the prediction come true – Macbeth thinks of that *all on his own*.

BANQUO
Look, how our partner's rapt. (1.3.9)

Macbeth
Shmoop Learning Guide

Thought: This is the second time Banquo has described Macbeth as being "rapt" after the witches make their prediction. Clearly, Macbeth is *really* interested in what the weird sisters have said and the use of the word "rapt" is a pretty accurate way to describe how Macbeth is absorbed in his thoughts (as in the passage above). At the same time, there's also a suggestion that Macbeth is in a kind of trance, which implies that he has no control over himself (his thoughts, his actions, etc.).

MACBETH
[Aside] If chance will have me king, why, chance may crown me,
Without my stir. (1.3.10)

Thought: Here, Macbeth seems content to leave his future to "chance." If "chance" will have him crowned king, then there's no reason for Macbeth to "stir" or lift a finger against King Duncan (or anyone else) in order to make things happen.

MACBETH
[Aside] The Prince of Cumberland! that is a step
On which I must fall down, or else o'erleap,
For in my way it lies. Stars, hide your fires;
Let not light see my black and deep desires:
The eye wink at the hand; yet let that be,
Which the eye fears, when it is done, to see. (1.4.4)

Thought: Uh, oh. Back at 1.3.10 (above), Macbeth seemed content to sit back and let his fate unfold. But, once he learns that King Duncan has named Malcolm the Prince of Cumberland and heir to the crown of Scotland, Macbeth decides that he must take action or, "o'erleap" what now appears to obstruct his path to the throne. He acknowledges that his "desires" are "black and deep" so it's obvious that he's decided to commit murder in order to make the witches' prophesy come true. Hmm. Macbeth seems willful at this moment.

MACBETH
We will proceed no further in this business:
He hath honour'd me of late; and I have bought
Golden opinions from all sorts of people,
Which would be worn now in their newest gloss,
Not cast aside so soon.
LADY MACBETH
Was the hope drunk
Wherein you dress'd yourself? hath it slept since?
And wakes it now, to look so green and pale
At what it did so freely? From this time
Such I account thy love. Art thou afeard
To be the same in thine own act and valour
As thou art in desire? Wouldst thou have that

Macbeth
Shmoop Learning Guide

Which thou esteem'st the ornament of life,
And live a coward in thine own esteem,
Letting 'I dare not' wait upon 'I would,'
Like the poor cat i' the adage?
MACBETH
Prithee, peace:
I dare do all that may become a man;
Who dares do more is none. (1.7.3)

Thought: Macbeth waffles here about killing King Duncan and insists that the murder plot is off. But, Lady Macbeth isn't having any of this and browbeats her husband until he changes his mind. Here, it seems that Macbeth makes another *deliberate choice*. He doesn't want his wife to think he's a "coward" so he says he'll "do all that may become a man." For more on the implications of Lady Macbeth's attack on her husband's masculinity, see "Quotes" for "Gender."

Is this a dagger which I see before me,
The handle toward my hand? Come, let me clutch thee.
I have thee not, and yet I see thee still.
Art thou not, fatal vision, sensible
To feeling as to sight? or art thou but
A dagger of the mind, a false creation,
Proceeding from the heat-oppressed brain?
I see thee yet, in form as palpable
As this which now I draw.
Thou marshall'st me the way that I was going;
And such an instrument I was to use. (2.1.1)

Thought: When Macbeth sees an imaginary floating dagger that points him in the direction of the sleeping King's room, we wonder if Macbeth has any control over whether or not he follows the apparition and, in doing so, *follows through* with the murder of Duncan. What do *you* think is going on here?

MACBETH
If't be so,
For Banquo's issue have I fil'd my mind,
For them the gracious Duncan have I murther'd,
Put rancors in the vessel of my peace
Only for them, and mine eternal jewel
Given to the common enemy of man,
To make them kings -the seed of Banquo kings!
Rather than so, come, Fate, into the list,
And champion me to the utterance! (3.1.8)

Macbeth
Shmoop Learning Guide

Thought: After murdering Duncan and being crowned king, Macbeth is not content, especially when he considers that the witches' prophesy (back in Act I, scene iii) also included a prediction that Banquo's heirs would one day be kings. Macbeth is determined to prevent that from happening and here, he openly challenges "Fate." Now that's interesting, don't you think?

Macbeth's use of language is interesting too. A soldier at heart, he invites Fate "into the list," suggesting that his struggle against a predetermined future is like fighting in man-to-man combat. Hmm. Seems a little arrogant. You might want to compare this passage to 1.2.1 (above), where the Captain says that Macbeth "disdain[ed] Fortune" as he fought against Macdonwald.

Third Apparition
Be lion-mettled, proud; and take no care
Who chafes, who frets, or where conspirers are:
Macbeth shall never vanquish'd be until
Great Birnam wood to high Dunsinane hill
Shall come against him.
 Descends
MACBETH
That will never be
Who can impress the forest, bid the tree
Unfix his earth-bound root? Sweet bodements! good!
Rebellion's head, rise never till the wood
Of Birnam rise, and our high-placed Macbeth
Shall live the lease of nature, pay his breath
To time and mortal custom. (4.1.1)

Thought: When Macbeth visits the weird sisters for more details about his future, Shakespeare's witches whip up a magic brew and conjure three apparitions that correctly predict what is to come. What's interesting about Act IV, Scene i, is that the apparitions offer predictions in the form of riddles that trick Macbeth into thinking he will be safe. Here, for example, the Third Apparition says that Macbeth will be safe so long as Birnam Wood never moves to Dunsinane. Macbeth's pretty certain that a grove of trees can't possible uproot themselves so he's confident at this point. Yet, we know that, in the end, Malcolm orders his armed troops to cut branches from the trees at Birnam Wood to use as camouflage as they advance toward the castle. So, what are we to make of this? The witches seem to know exactly what will happen to Macbeth. So, why do they go out of their way to trick him into believing something (that he's safe) that will undoubtedly influence the *decisions* he will make about how to prepare for battle. Are Macbeth's *decisions* and *actions* the things that determine his outcome? Or, is it something else?

Ambition Quotes

Macbeth
Shmoop Learning Guide

BANQUO
*[…] My noble partner
You greet with present grace and great prediction
Of noble having and of royal hope,
That he seems rapt withal. To me you speak not.
If you can look into the seeds of time,
And say which grain will grow and which will not,
Speak then to me, who neither beg nor fear
Your favors nor your hate. (1.3.2)*

Thought: After hearing the witches predict that Macbeth will be Thane of Cawdor and King of Scotland, Banquo notes that his friend is "rapt withal," suggesting that Macbeth is consumed or entranced by the prophecy. Banquo is eager to hear what the witches have in store for him and we can see that Banquo is ambitious – he's pleased as punch when he learns his heirs will be kings (even though he will never wear the crown). Yet, Banquo *never* takes drastic measures to gain power for himself or his heirs, which makes him a foil to Macbeth who, eventually, will stop at nothing to secure his power.

MACBETH
*My thought, whose murder yet is but fantastical,
Shakes so my single state of man that function
Is smother'd in surmise, and nothing is
But what is not. (1.3.9)*

Thought: After the weird sisters predict that Macbeth will be king, his thoughts turn to "murder," which the sisters have said *nothing* about. Could it be that the witches' prophesy awakens within Macbeth a murderous ambition that was there all along?

MACBETH
*[Aside] The Prince of Cumberland! That is a step
On which I must fall down, or else o'erleap,
For in my way it lies. Stars, hide your fires;
Let not light see my black and deep desires.
The eye wink at the hand; yet let that be
Which the eye fears, when it is done, to see. (1.4.4)*

Thought: By the time Malcolm is proclaimed Prince of Cumberland and heir to the throne of Scotland, Macbeth is willing to push all morality aside. He knows that killing Duncan in order to become king is wrong, which is why he says it's necessary to hide his "black and deep" desires. Here, ambition is portrayed as something dark and ugly.

Macbeth
Shmoop Learning Guide

LADY MACBETH
[...]
Glamis thou art, and Cawdor; and shalt be
What thou art promised: yet do I fear thy nature;
It is too full o' the milk of human kindness
To catch the nearest way: thou wouldst be great;
Art not without ambition, but without
The illness should attend it: (1.5.1)

Thought: After reading the letter from her husband (which recounts the witches' prophesy), Lady Macbeth's thoughts immediately turn to murder. In her mind, Macbeth must take action if he is to become king. Macbeth, she says, is certainly not without "ambition." The problem, as Lady Macbeth sees it, is that her husband is too "kind" to do what's necessary to achieve "great[ness]."

MACBETH
[...] I have no spur
To prick the sides of my intent, but only
Vaulting ambition, which o'erleaps itself
And falls on the other. (1.7.1)

Thought: As Macbeth deliberates, he realizes that "vaulting ambition" is all that compels him to the heinous act of murdering Duncan and that his intent is nothing but personal gain. This is not enough to justify the act of killing a king, which is why he resolves to not go through with it after this speech. Of course, we know that Macbeth (with some encouragement from his wife) *does* murder Duncan.

ROSS
'Gainst nature still!
Thriftless ambition, that wilt ravin up
Thine own life's means! Then 'tis most like
The sovereignty will fall upon Macbeth. (2.4.6)

Thought: At first, everyone assumes that Duncan's sons are responsible for his murder. (Having fled the castle after Duncan's body was discovered, Malcolm and Donalbain appear guilty.) Here, Ross implies that ambition leads to the most unnatural acts as he accuses Duncan's sons of being "ambition" personified. Ambition, he suggests, is a cannibal that goes "'gainst nature" to kill its father and "raven up" or, devour the very man who gave it life.

If Ross knew that Macbeth was the man responsible for the murder, would his response be any different than what he says here?

Macbeth
Shmoop Learning Guide

BANQUO
Thou hast it now: King, Cawdor, Glamis, all,
As the weird women promised, and I fear
Thou play'dst most foully for't; yet it was said
It should not stand in thy posterity,
But that myself should be the root and father
Of many kings. If there come truth from them
(As upon thee, Macbeth, their speeches shine)
Why, by the verities on thee made good,
May they not be my oracles as well
And set me up in hope? But hush, no more. (3.1.1)

Thought: Earlier, we suggested that Banquo seems to be an honorable guy because, unlike Macbeth, he doesn't murder anyone for self gain. Yet, here, one could argue that Banquo might as well be an accomplice to the King's murder. Though he suspects Macbeth of foul play, he doesn't say a word to anybody. Could it be that his own ambitions prevent him from outing or confronting Macbeth? What do you think?

MACBETH
[…] For mine own good
All causes shall give way. I am in blood
Stepp'd in so far that, should I wade no more,
Returning were as tedious as go o'er. (3.4.24)

Thought: By comparing his heinous actions to wading through a bloody river, Macbeth suggests that once a man commits a murderous act for his own gain, it's impossible to stop. Turning back would be "tedious." By this point, Macbeth is willing to *anything* in order to help himself and it's becomes easier for him to commit evil deeds. According to Macbeth, he's got to look out for his own best interests.

MACDUFF
[…] Either thou, Macbeth,
Or else my sword, with an unbatter'd edge,
I sheathe again undeeded. There thou shouldst be;
By this great clatter, one of greatest note
Seems bruited. Let me find him, Fortune!
And more I beg not. (5.8.1)

Thought: Macduff's only ambition is to kill Macbeth, the man who has murdered his wife and children. He has no interest in personal gain and is the first character in the play to understand that Fortune rules you, you don't rule Fortune. This is a certain indicator that he'll be the one to take down the tyrant, who is always challenging destiny. (Check out "Quotes" for "Fate and Free Will" for more about this.)

Macbeth
Shmoop Learning Guide

MACBETH
[...]
Wherefore was that cry?
SEYTON
The queen, my lord, is dead.
MACBETH
She should have died hereafter;
There would have been a time for such a word.
To-morrow, and to-morrow, and to-morrow,
Creeps in this petty pace from day to day
To the last syllable of recorded time
And all our yesterdays have lighted fools
The way to dusty death. Out, out, brief candle!
Life's but a walking shadow, a poor player
That struts and frets his hour upon the stage
And then is heard no more: it is a tale
Told by an idiot, full of sound and fury,
Signifying nothing. (5.5.2)

Thought: The story of Macbeth and his wife serves as a cautionary tale for the overly ambitious. By the play's end, the once power hungry Lady Macbeth is plagued with guilt and turns to suicide. Macbeth's response to the news of his wife's death is just as bleak. The words "to-morrow, and, to-morrow, and to-morrow" suggest that the world has lost all meaning for him. He says life is a "tale" "full of sound and fury" and, ultimately, the story signifies "nothing." In the end, Macbeth sees himself as nothing more than a character in a story that has absolutely no meaning, which is a pretty depressing point of view.

Of course, this reminds the audience that these words are being spoken by an actor on stage. This self-conscious moment is pretty typical of Shakespeare, who often reflects on the workings of the theater in his plays. In *As You Like It*, Jaques says something quite similar: "All the world's a stage/ And all the men and women merely players"(2.2.139). The difference between *Macbeth* and *As You Like It*, however, is that Jaques, an amused cynic, seems to take some pleasure in the similarities between the theater and the world. Here, Macbeth is full of despair.

FYI: This passage inspired the title of William Faulkner's *The Sound and the Fury*.

Power Quotes

Third Witch
All hail, Macbeth, thou shalt be king hereafter!
[...]
Thou shalt get kings, though thou be none:
So all hail, Macbeth and Banquo! (1.3.4-6)

Macbeth
Shmoop Learning Guide

Thought: The witches prediction that Macbeth will become monarch and that Banquo's heirs will be future kings sets the plot in motion. Up until this point, Macbeth doesn't seem to have kingly aspirations. In fact, he's just returning home from successfully defending King Duncan against Scottish traitors and the Norwegian King's armed forces.

This moment also lays the groundwork for Shakespeare's portrayal of the Stuart political myth. King James I of England (a.k.a. King James VI of Scotland) was the current monarch when Shakespeare wrote *Macbeth* (around 1606) and he traced his lineage back to Banquo, the man who "shalt get kings." We'll definitely want to keep an eye on how Shakespeare portrays James's supposed ancestor.

MACBETH
[...]
If good, why do I yield to that suggestion
Whose horrid image doth unfix my hair
And make my seated heart knock at my ribs,
Against the use of nature? Present fears
Are less than horrible imaginings:
My thought, whose murder yet is but fantastical,
Shakes so my single state of man that function
Is smother'd in surmise, and nothing is
But what is not. (1.3.9)

Thought: The first time Macbeth's thoughts turn to murdering King Duncan (in order to fulfill the witches' prophesy), he's terrified by his own "horrible imaginings." Murder in itself is enough to "shake" Macbeth but the idea of murdering a king (regicide) is particularly awful.

History Snack: Regicide was a pretty common occurrence in 11th century Scotland (the setting of *Macbeth*) but the idea of murdering a king would have been particularly startling for Shakespeare's 17th century audience. King James was a big fan of a theory called the "Divine Right of Kings," which said that monarchs were God's appointed representatives on earth and that rebelling against the monarch was an affront to God. James even wrote about it in The Trew Law of Free Monarchies (1598), where he claimed that "The state of monarchy is the supremest thing upon earth; for kings are not only God's lieutenants upon earth, and sit upon God's throne, but even by God himself are called gods."

DUNCAN
My plenteous joys,
Wanton in fulness, seek to hide themselves
In drops of sorrow. Sons, kinsmen, thanes,
And you whose places are the nearest, know
We will establish our estate upon
Our eldest, Malcolm, whom we name hereafter
The Prince of Cumberland; which honour must
Not unaccompanied invest him only,

Macbeth
Shmoop Learning Guide

*But signs of nobleness, like stars, shall shine
On all deservers. From hence to Inverness,
And bind us further to you. (1.4.4)*

Thought: When King Duncan names his son, Malcolm, the Prince of Cumberland, he's essentially naming him the heir apparent to the throne. (Note: At the time, Scotland was *not* a hereditary monarchy – it was elective so Duncan's technically out of line here.) At this point, Macbeth decides that Malcolm and King Duncan are a serious obstacle in his path to the throne – "The Prince of Cumberland! that is a step / On which I must fall down, or else o'erleap, / For in my way it lies" (1.4.4).

MACBETH
[…]
*Besides, this Duncan
Hath borne his faculties so meek, hath been
So clear in his great office, that his virtues
Will plead like angels, trumpet-tongued, against
The deep damnation of his taking-off;*
(1.7.1)

Thought: As Macbeth deliberates about whether or not his plans to kill Duncan is justifiable, he notes that Duncan is a virtuous king so nobody in their right mind would say it's OK to murder him. In Shakespeare's major source for the play, Holinshed's *Chronicles*, King Duncan is a young and weak ruler and although Shakespeare makes Duncan into an older and benevolent king in *Macbeth*, he also seems to imply that Duncan is a bit too soft. Here, Macbeth describes him as "meek" and we already know that the king is way too trusting. It seems that Shakespeare sets up Duncan as the polar opposite of what Macbeth will become when he's crowned King. Is Shakespeare suggesting that a good monarch should inhabit a space somewhere in between "meekness" and tyranny? Or, is Duncan a model of ideal kingship?

PORTER
[…]
*Knock,
knock! Who's there, in the other devil's
name? Faith, here's an equivocator, that could
swear in both the scales against either scale;
who committed treason enough for God's sake,
yet could not equivocate to heaven: O, come
in, equivocator. (2.3.1)*

Thought: After Macbeth murders King Duncan while the monarch sleeps (as a guest at Macbeth's castle), there's knocking at the castle's gates. Here, the drunken Porter (whose comedic antics inject a bit of levity into the play) imagines who could be knocking at such an hour. Here, he pretends there's an "equivocator" at the door. (Generally speaking, an "equivocator" is a person who speaks ambiguously or doesn't tell the whole truth.) This is likely

Macbeth
Shmoop Learning Guide

a reference to Jesuit Henry Garnet, a man who was tried and executed for his role in the Gunpowder Plot of 1605 (an unsuccessful attempt by a group of Catholic extremists to blow up Parliament and King James I with a keg of gunpowder). Henry Garnet happens to be the guy who wrote the "Treatise on Equivocation," which encouraged Catholics to speak ambiguously or, "equivocate" when they were being questioned by Protestant inquisitors (so they wouldn't be persecuted for their religious beliefs). He also did a lot of "equivocating" when he stood trial.

Even though the Porter is joking, the jest comes at a significant moment in the play. Macbeth, as we've said, has just murdered Duncan. Dramatizing the murder of a king on stage was a pretty dangerous thing for Shakespeare to do, but the reference to the Gunpowder Plot is also a very clear condemnation of the crime Macbeth has just committed.

ROSS
Ah, good father,
Thou seest, the heavens, as troubled with man's act,
Threaten his bloody stage: by the clock, 'tis day,
And yet dark night strangles the travelling lamp:
Is't night's predominance, or the day's shame,
That darkness does the face of earth entomb,
When living light should kiss it?
Old Man
'Tis unnatural,
Even like the deed that's done. (2.4.1)

Thought: The day after King Duncan's murder, Ross notes that nature has responded, in an "unnatural" way, to the king's murder. Even though it's the middle of the day, darkness fills the sky, as though the sun ("the traveling lamp") has been "strangle[d]" by "dark night." Given that kings are frequently associated with the sun's power, this is an especially apt metaphor. Duncan's rule *and* his life have both been *extinguished* by Macbeth, who has committed the most "unnatural" act of all.

LORD
The son of Duncan,
From whom this tyrant holds the due of birth
[…] (3.6.1)

Thought: It's not long after Macbeth is crowned king that he's viewed as a "tyrant" who has deprived Duncan's son, Malcolm (who was named heir before his father's murder), of his "due of birth." As we've said before, Scotland was not, at this time, a hereditary monarch (it was elective) so there's a bit of a discrepancy here.

What to make of this? The play seems invested in asserting that the stability of the throne (and the kingdom) rests upon patrilineal succession (when the crown is passed from father to eldest son). Macbeth's crime, then, is not merely regicide – he's also disrupted the royal line, which must be righted before the play's end.

Macbeth
Shmoop Learning Guide

LORD
The son of Duncan
[...]
Lives in the English court, and is received
Of the most pious Edward with such grace
That the malevolence of fortune nothing
Takes from his high respect: thither Macduff
Is gone to pray the holy king, upon his aid
To wake Northumberland and warlike Siward:
That, by the help of these--with Him above
To ratify the work--we may again
Give to our tables meat, sleep to our nights,
Free from our feasts and banquets bloody knives,
Do faithful homage and receive free honours:
All which we pine for now: and this report
Hath so exasperate the king that he
Prepares for some attempt of war. (3.6.1)

Thought: It seems that Shakespeare can't resist giving the English king, Edward the Confessor (c. 1003-1066) some props in this Scottish play. Malcolm has fled to England, seeking refuge from Macbeth and help from King Edward. The "pious Edward," of course, stands in contrast to the tyrant Macbeth and Edward's aid will play a major role in the restoration of political order in Scotland. A few lines later, Lennox prays that a "swift blessing" (help from the English army) will alleviate Scotland's "suffering" under Macbeth's "accursed" hand (3.6.3).

MACBETH
Thou art too like the spirit of Banquo: down!
Thy crown does sear mine eye-balls. And thy hair,
Thou other gold-bound brow, is like the first.
A third is like the former. Filthy hags!
Why do you show me this? A fourth! Start, eyes!
What, will the line stretch out to the crack of doom?
Another yet! A seventh! I'll see no more:
And yet the eighth appears, who bears a glass
Which shows me many more; and some I see
That two-fold balls and treble scepters carry:
Horrible sight! Now, I see, 'tis true;
For the blood-bolter'd Banquo smiles upon me,
And points at them for his. (4.1.8)

Thought: Macbeth is *not* pleased when the witches conjure a vision of eight kings, the last of which holds a mirror that reflects on many more such kings. These are Banquo's heirs, which will one day rule Scotland. One of the kings in the mirror happens to be holding two orbs, an obvious nod to King James. As we've said before, King James I of England (a.k.a. King James

Macbeth
Shmoop Learning Guide

VI of Scotland) traced his lineage back to Banquo and, at his coronation ceremony in England (1603), James held two orbs (one representing England and one representing Scotland). Shakespeare seems to be flattering here, don't you think?

DOCTOR
Ay, sir; there are a crew of wretched souls
That stay his cure: their malady convinces
The great assay of art; but at his touch--
Such sanctity hath heaven given his hand--
They presently amend.
[…]
MALCOLM
'Tis call'd the evil:
A most miraculous work in this good king;
Which often, since my here-remain in England,
I have seen him do. How he solicits heaven,
Himself best knows: but strangely-visited people,
All swoln and ulcerous, pitiful to the eye,
The mere despair of surgery, he cures,
Hanging a golden stamp about their necks,
Put on with holy prayers: and 'tis spoken,
To the succeeding royalty he leaves
The healing benediction. With this strange virtue,
He hath a heavenly gift of prophecy,
And sundry blessings hang about his throne,
That speak him full of grace. (4.3.1)

Thought: Shakespeare gives more props to King Edward the Confessor of England. This passage is an allusion to the "Royal Touch," a kind of laying on hands ceremony that was performed by English (and French) monarchs. It was thought to have been started by King Edward. The "wretched souls" referred to here by the Doctor suffer from Scrofula or, the "King's Evil," what we now know is a form of tuberculosis that affects the lymph nodes and skin. In a book called *The Royal Touch*, historian Marc Bloch writes that King James I (who sat on the throne when *Macbeth* was first written and performed) wasn't exactly thrilled about performing this ceremony – he thought it was superstitious and silly – but he did it anyway to make his subjects happy.

So, if King Edward can cure a nasty disease like Scrofula, just imagine what he can do to help cure Scotland of Macbeth…

Versions of Reality Quotes

ALL
Fair is foul, and foul is fair.
Hover through the fog and filthy air. (1.1.1)

Macbeth
Shmoop Learning Guide

Thought: The witches' chant, "fair is foul and foul is fair," reverberates throughout the entire play. Appearances can be deceiving and the difference between reality and illusion, good and evil, etc. is often as murky as the "fog and filthy air."

MACBETH
So foul and fair a day I have not seen. (1.3.1)

Thought: Hmm. This sounds familiar. Didn't the weird sisters just say something similar? Does Macbeth already have some kind of psychic connection with the weird sisters?

DUNCAN
There's no art
To find the mind's construction in the face:
He was a gentleman on whom I built
An absolute trust. (1.4.2)

Thought: Here, King Duncan says that the former Thane of Cawdor (who turned out to be a traitor) *seemed* to be a "gentleman" he could "trust." His insistence that it's impossible to know a man's mind by reading his "face" suggests that Duncan has learned his lesson because he acknowledges that outside appearances cannot be banked on. Yet, he makes the exact same mistake when he names Macbeth Thane of Cawdor and puts his faith in the man who will eventually murder him.

LADY MACBETH
Your face, my Thane, is as a book where men
May read strange matters. To beguile the time,
Look like the time; bear welcome in your eye,
Your hand, your tongue; look like the innocent flower,
But be the serpent under it. (1.5.5)

Thought: Lady Macbeth seems shrewd here. Here, she echoes King Duncan's comments that it's hard to judge a man by outward appearances (see 1.4.2 above). She notes that anyone could read Macbeth's "strange" thoughts, "like a book," by gazing at his "face." With this in mind, she encourages Macbeth to play the gracious host while pretending to be as innocent as a "flower."

DUNCAN
See, see, our honour'd hostess!
The love that follows us sometime is our trouble,
Which still we thank as love.
[…]
Fair and noble hostess,
We are your guest to-night. (1.6.2-3)

Macbeth
Shmoop Learning Guide

Thought: Lady Macbeth welcomes King Duncan to the castle and she's incredibly charming. When Duncan calls her a "*fair* and noble hostess," we're reminded of the witches' mantra, "fair is foul and foul is fair" (see 1.1.1 above). Lady Macbeth, as we know, intends to help her husband murder Duncan in his sleep, which is decidedly *un*gracious.

MACBETH
I am settled and bend up
Each corporal agent to this terrible feat.
Away, and mock the time with fairest show:
False face must hide what the false heart doth know. (1.7.7)

Thought: Here, Macbeth resolves to murder the King. He is attempting to convince himself as much as anyone else by putting up a front. He says his false face will hide from others his plan to murder Duncan, but knowing what we know, he might also be convincing his false face to fool his own heart.

MACBETH
Is this a dagger which I see before me,
The handle toward my hand? Come, let me clutch thee.
I have thee not, and yet I see thee still.
Art thou not, fatal vision, sensible
To feeling as to sight? Or art thou but
A dagger of the mind, a false creation,
Proceeding from the heat-oppressed brain?
I see thee yet, in form as palpable
As this which now I draw.
Thou marshal'st me the way that I was going,
And such an instrument I was to use.
Mine eyes are made the fools o' the other senses,
Or else worth all the rest. (2.1.6)

Thought: As Macbeth prepares to murder Duncan, he sees a "dagger of the mind" floating in mid air. The dagger points in the direction of the room where the king sleeps – clearly, the dagger represents the murder Macbeth is about to commit. The question is, who or what is responsible for conjuring this image? The witches? Some other outside force? Or, is this a product entirely of Macbeth's imagination? We also wonder whether or not it's meant to be a temptation or a warning.

MACDUFF
Malcolm and Donalbain, the King's two sons,
Are stol'n away and fled, which puts upon them
Suspicion of the deed.
ROSS
'Gainst nature still!

Macbeth
Shmoop Learning Guide

Thriftless ambition, that wilt ravin up
Thine own life's means! Then 'tis most like
The sovereignty will fall upon Macbeth. (2.4.3)

Thought: Although it appears that Duncan's sons are guilty of bribing the guards to murder their father, the audience knows Macbeth is really at fault. Here, what seems to be "fair" (Macbeth) is "foul" and what appears to be "foul" (Duncan's sons) is really "fair." Interestingly enough, Ross's words ring true, not of Donalbain and Malcolm, but of Macbeth, who *is* in fact guilty of "thriftless ambition."

LADY MACBETH
O proper stuff!
This is the very painting of your fear:
This is the air-drawn dagger which, you said,
Led you to Duncan. O, these flaws and starts,
Impostors to true fear, would well become
A woman's story at a winter's fire,
Authorized by her grandam. Shame itself!
Why do you make such faces? When all's done,
You look but on a stool. (3.4.4)

Thought: Uh oh. It looks like somebody's got a guilty conscious. Macbeth is the only character in the play who sees the ghost of Banquo at the dinner feast. (As we know, Macbeth ordered Banquo's murder and also tried to have Fleance killed.) So, what's going on here? Is Macbeth losing his mind? Is the ghost real? (It wasn't uncommon for ghosts to appear to a selective audience in the literature of the period.) Or, has Macbeth conjured the apparition? If you want to think about the implications of Lady Macbeth's insistence that Macbeth is acting like an old *woman* telling ghost stories around a campfire, check out "Quotes" for "Gender."

FIRST APPARITION [an armed head]
Macbeth! Macbeth! Macbeth! Beware Macduff,
Beware the Thane of Fife. Dismiss me. Enough. (4.1.1)

Thought: Macbeth is blinded by what he *wants* to see. The head presented to him is clearly his own, warning him of his own demise at the hands of Macduff. (In the last scene, Macduff presents Macbeth's severed head to Malcolm.) Macbeth doesn't read the signs, or even look for them, because he is so consumed by his own immediate desires.

MALCOLM
It is myself I mean: in whom I know
All the particulars of vice so grafted
That, when they shall be open'd, black Macbeth
Will seem as pure as snow, and the poor state
Esteem him as a lamb, being compared

Macbeth
Shmoop Learning Guide

With my confineless harms.
MACDUFF
Not in the legions
Of horrid hell can come a devil more damn'd
In evils to top Macbeth.
(4.3.6)

Thought: Macduff has all of the appearances of a traitor, when in fact his intentions are noble. Here, he pretends that he will be as tyrannous as Macbeth when he is crowned king, much to Macduff's horror. Eventually he confesses to Macduff that he is only testing the man's loyalty to Scotland.

Gentlewoman
It is an accustomed action with her, to seem thus
washing her hands: I have known her continue in
this a quarter of an hour.
LADY MACBETH
Yet here's a spot. (5.1.5)

Thought: At the end of her life, Lady Macbeth has lost her mind – she sleepwalks throughout the castle and compulsively washes the imaginary blood from her hands. Ironically, this recalls Lady Macbeth's earlier insistence that "A little water clears us of this deed: / How easy is it, then!" (2.2.14), wouldn't you say? It may have been easy for the couple to clean up after killing Duncan but it becomes impossible for Lady Macbeth to erase her actions or even wash away her guilt.

Gender Quotes

BANQUO
You should be women,
And yet your beards forbid me to interpret
That you are so. (1.3.1)

Thought: Banquo's confusion about the witches' gender is pretty striking and speaks to the play's notion that the witches are "too masculine" to be women. (In 17th century England, the ideal woman was silent, obedient, chaste, beautiful, and submissive, etc. and the weird sisters are none of these things.) Like Lady Macbeth, who taunts her husband into killing Duncan by questioning his manhood, the witches are menacing figures that trigger Macbeth's murderous ambition, which brings about his ruin. Remember, it's their prophecy that leads Macbeth to first consider killing Duncan in order to secure his, Macbeth's, power. (On the other hand, we might also remember that the play goes out of its way to show that Macbeth makes his own decisions. The witches never say anything about murder – they just tell Macbeth he's going to become king.)

Macbeth
Shmoop Learning Guide

First Witch
I myself have all the other,
And the very ports they blow,
All the quarters that they know
I' the shipman's card.
I will drain him dry as hay:
Sleep shall neither night nor day
Hang upon his pent-house lid;
He shall live a man forbid:
Weary se'nnights nine times nine
Shall he dwindle, peak and pine:
Though his bark cannot be lost,
Yet it shall be tempest-tost.
Look what I have.
Second Witch
Show me, show me.
First Witch
Here I have a pilot's thumb,
Wreck'd as homeward he did come. (1.3.4)

Thought: Here, the First Witch describes how she's going to punish a sailor's wife (who refused to share some of her chestnuts) by whipping up a nasty little storm so the sailor's ship, currently at sea, will be "tempest-tost." What's more, she says she's going to "drain [the sailor] dry as hay," which means that she's going to make the sailor impotent (so he can't have children). Fear of male impotency is something that surfaces in the play over and over again. (Even the Porter jokes about it in Act II, scene iii.) Most notably, Lady Macbeth, who is often aligned with the witches, implies that her husband is unable to perform sexually (see 1.7.3 below) when he refuses to kill Duncan.

Glamis thou art, and Cawdor; and shalt be
What thou art promised: yet do I fear thy nature;
It is too full o' the milk of human kindness
To catch the nearest way: thou wouldst be great;
Art not without ambition, but without
The illness should attend it:
[…]
Hie thee hither,
That I may pour my spirits in thine ear;
And chastise with the valour of my tongue
All that impedes thee from the golden round,
Which fate and metaphysical aid doth seem
To have thee crown'd withal.
(1.5.1)

Macbeth
Shmoop Learning Guide

Thought: According to Lady Macbeth, her husband is ambitious, but he is also too "kind" to do what it takes to murder Duncan so that he, Macbeth, can be king. What's a wife to do? Lady Macbeth plans to "chastise" Macbeth with the "valour of [her] tongue," which is another way of saying she's going to browbeat her husband into taking action so he can be "crown'd withal." This speech establishes Lady Macbeth as the dominant partner in the relationship, which inverts typical 17th century gender and social roles. (Husbands were supposed to "rule" their wives in the same way that kings ruled countries.)

LADY MACBETH
[...] Come, you spirits
That tend on mortal thoughts, unsex me here,
And fill me from the crown to the toe top-full
Of direst cruelty! make thick my blood;
Stop up the access and passage to remorse,
That no compunctious visitings of nature
Shake my fell purpose, nor keep peace between
The effect and it! Come to my woman's breasts,
And take my milk for gall, you murdering ministers,
Wherever in your sightless substances
You wait on nature's mischief! Come, thick night,
And pall thee in the dunnest smoke of hell,
That my keen knife see not the wound it makes,
Nor heaven peep through the blanket of the dark,
To cry 'Hold, hold!' (1.5.3)

Thought: In the previous passage we saw that Lady Macbeth thinks her husband doesn't have it in him to do what it takes to become king (murder Duncan). Here, she psyches herself up to help Macbeth by calling on "spirits" to "unsex" her – to stop her menstrual flow ("make thick [her] blood" and "stop the visitings of nature") and to change her breast "milk" for poison or, "gall" – all things that make her a reproductive woman with the capacity for nurture.

So, why would Lady Macbeth want to be rendered sterile? This passage suggests that, for Lady Macbeth, being a reproductive woman could prevent her from committing a violent deed. It seems that Lady Macbeth construes femininity as compassion and "kindness" and also believes that masculinity is synonymous with "direst cruelty." So, when Lady Macbeth says earlier (1.5.1 above) that Macbeth is "too full o' the *milk* of human *kindness*," she's essentially saying that Macbeth is too much like a woman (1.5.1).

LADY MACBETH
Was the hope drunk
Wherein you dress'd yourself? hath it slept since?
And wakes it now, to look so green and pale
At what it did so freely? From this time
Such I account thy love. Art thou afeard
To be the same in thine own act and valour

Macbeth
Shmoop Learning Guide

As thou art in desire? Wouldst thou have that
Which thou esteem'st the ornament of life,
And live a coward in thine own esteem,
Letting 'I dare not' wait upon 'I would,'
Like the poor cat i' the adage?
MACBETH
Prithee, peace:
I dare do all that may become a man;
Who dares do more is none.
LADY MACBETH
What beast was't, then,
That made you break this enterprise to me?
When you durst do it, then you were a man; (1.7.3)

Thought: True to her word, Lady Macbeth gives her husband a tongue lashing when he hesitates about killing King Duncan. She calls him a "coward" and says "When you durst do it, *then* you were a man." Pretty emasculating, wouldn't you say?

We're also interested in the way Lady Macbeth implies that "doing" the deed (killing Duncan) is like "doing" what a man does in the bedroom. She asks "Art thou afeard / To be the same in thine own act and valour / As thou art in desire"? Translation: Are you afraid you'll be as impotent in the act of killing the king as you are during sex ("desire")? Macbeth insists that he can "do *all* that may become a man," he attempts to reassert his manhood in the face of Lady Macbeth's belittling comments.

LADY MACBETH
I have given suck and know
How tender 'tis to love the babe that milks me-
I would, while it was smiling in my face,
Have pluck'd my nipple from his boneless gums
And dash'd the brains out had I so sworn as you
Have done to this. (1.7.3)

Thought: Lady Macbeth sure knows how to conjure up some violent imagery, doesn't she? After she browbeats her husband into saying that he'll go ahead with the murder of the king, she goes on (famously) to insist that, if she had promised to do so, she'd tear her nursing child from her breast and "dash" its "brains out." Yikes! We can link this passage back to Lady Macbeth's earlier remarks about "the milk of human kindness" being synonymous with femininity and "direst cruelty" being associated with masculinity (see above passages).

MACBETH
Bring forth men-children only,
For thy undaunted mettle should compose
Nothing but males. (1.7.6)

Macbeth
Shmoop Learning Guide

Thought: Macbeth acknowledges his wife's strength and power by suggesting that it would be fitting if she gave birth to "men-children only." Her "undaunted mettle" suggests that she has all the makings of a strong and brave man. Of course, Lady Macbeth won't be giving birth to *any* children after this, which is one of the play's most important points – from this point on, Macbeth's marriage is sterile. Unlike Banquo (who will beget kings), Macbeth will never sire heirs that will be monarchs and this is deeply upsetting to him. Later, Macbeth laments that when the witches made their prophecy, they "placed a *fruitless* crown" upon his head and put a "*barren* scepter" in his hands (3.1.8).

MACDUFF
O gentle lady,
'Tis not for you to hear what I can speak:
The repetition in a woman's ear
Would murder as it fell. (2.3.12)

Thought: When Lady Macbeth enters the room and demands to know what's happened (as if she has no idea her husband just murdered the king), Macduff refuses to explain. He assumes that women are far too delicate for such matters. Not only that, but Macduff assumes that Lady Macbeth, being a *lady*, is above suspicion.

LADY MACBETH
What's to be done?
MACBETH
Be innocent of the knowledge, dearest chuck,
Till thou applaud the deed. (3.2.6)

Thought: This is a major turning point in the relationship between Lady Macbeth and her husband. It's the first time Macbeth, who seems to have taken all of Lady Macbeth's chiding about his manhood to heart, excludes his wife from the decision making. He's planning to have Banquo murdered but he insists that Lady Macbeth be "innocent," that is, until he decides to let her in on his secret. *Then* she, "his "dearest chuck," can be cheerleader to his heroic "deed." This is where the two are beginning to drift apart.

LADY MACBETH
Are you a man?
[...]
O proper stuff!
This is the very painting of your fear;
This is the air-drawn dagger which you said
Led you to Duncan. O, these flaws and starts,
Impostors to true fear, would well become
A woman's story at a winter's fire,
Authorized by her grandam. Shame itself!
Why do you make such faces? When all's done,

Macbeth
Shmoop Learning Guide

You look but on a stool. (3.4.59)

Thought: Although we've just seen Macbeth assert himself as the dominant figure in the marriage (3.2.6), his frantic response to the appearance of Banquo's ghost is taken as a sign of weakness. (It appears that Macbeth is the only character who sees the apparition during the banquet.) Lady Macbeth reduces her husband's claim (that he's seen something terrifying) to an old lady's ghost story. This, as we later see in 5.1.2 (below), will come back to haunt her (pun intended).

MACBETH
What man dare, I dare:
Approach thou like the rugged Russian bear,
The arm'd rhinoceros, or the Hyrcan tiger;
Take any shape but that, and my firm nerves
Shall never tremble: or be alive again,
And dare me to the desert with thy sword;
If trembling I inhabit then, protest me
The baby of a girl. Hence, horrible shadow!
Unreal mockery, hence!
 GHOST OF BANQUO vanishes
Why, so: being gone,
I am a man again. Pray you, sit still. (3.4.20)

Thought: In the play, terror and masculinity cannot coexist. Here, Macbeth says that the only thing that makes him "tremble" like a "baby of a girl" (a baby girl and/or her doll) is the ghost of Banquo, which shakes him to his core. As soon as the apparition disappears, Macbeth feels as though he's a "man again."

MACDUFF
He has no children. All my pretty ones?
Did you say all? O hell-kite! All?
What, all my pretty chickens and their dam
At one fell swoop?
MALCOLM
Dispute it like a man.
MACDUFF
I shall do so,
But I must also feel it as a man.
I cannot but remember such things were
That were most precious to me. (4.3.26)

Thought: When Macduff learns that his wife and children have been murdered, Malcolm insists that he respond by fighting or "disput[ing]" the murder "like a man." In other words, he encourages Macduff to kill Macbeth, which, in Malcolm's mind, is synonymous with masculinity.

Macbeth
Shmoop Learning Guide

But, Macduff's *response* is unlike anything we've encountered in the play thus far. He says that, yes, he's going to pay back Macbeth but first, he's going to "feel" the loss of his family "as a man." According to Macduff, the capacity to "feel" (grief, love, and regret) are the things that make one a man, not cold-blooded apathy.

This is all the more striking when we contrast Macduff's words with the end of the play, where our protagonist, Macbeth, is incapable of any human emotion. He's unable to feel or express any grief over the death of his once beloved wife (5.5.3) and says he no longer feels any sense of "fear," despite his impending death (5.5.2). Macbeth, essentially, goes numb, which makes him seem like a mere shell of a man.

Gentlewoman
Since his majesty went into the field, I have seen
her rise from her bed, throw her night-gown upon
her, unlock her closet, take forth paper, fold it,
write upon't, read it, afterwards seal it, and again
return to bed; yet all this while in a most fast sleep.
Doctor
A great perturbation in nature, to receive at once
the benefit of sleep, and do the effects of
watching! In this slumbery agitation, besides her
walking and other actual performances, what, at any
time, have you heard her say? (5.1.2)

Thought: By the play's final act, Lady Macbeth has been reduced to an enfeebled woman who sleepwalks through the castle and mutters to herself as she attempts to wash the imaginary blood from her hands (5.1.6). We're struck by the way traditional gender roles are reestablished at the end of the play (unlike the beginning of the drama, where Lady Macbeth is a domineering figure who helps drive her husband to murder and kingship). By Act iii, scene iv, Lady Macbeth doesn't even appear on stage with her husband (off stage, she's surrounded by a group of gentlewomen who tend to her in her illness) and Macbeth says he has no time to think about his wife when he learns of her death (5.5.3). Lady Macbeth, who was once so central to the action of the play, is a pretty marginal character when all is said and done.

The Supernatural Quotes

Thunder and lightning. Enter three Witches
First Witch
When shall we three meet again
In thunder, lightning, or in rain?
Second Witch
When the hurlyburly's done,
When the battle's lost and won.
Third Witch
That will be ere the set of sun.

Macbeth
Shmoop Learning Guide

First Witch
Where the place?
Second Witch
Upon the heath.
Third Witch
There to meet with Macbeth.
First Witch
I come, Graymalkin!
Second Witch
Paddock calls.
Third Witch
Anon.
ALL
Fair is foul, and foul is fair:
Hover through the fog and filthy air. (1.1.1)

Thought: The witches' appearance in the play's opening scene certainly is dramatic but the sisters are also incredibly ambiguous. They seem to raise more questions than anything else. Who/what are they? (As readers, we're privy to the speech headings, which refer to the figures as witches but we can imagine what it would be like to witness this scene as an audience to a stage performance. The first witch refers to the crew simply as "we three" so their identity is unclear.) Where do they come from? What do they want with Macbeth? And, what do they have to do with the "battle"?

First Witch
A sailor's wife had chestnuts in her lap,
And munch'd, and munch'd, and munch'd:--
'Give me,' quoth I:
[...]
I myself have all the other,
And the very ports they blow,
All the quarters that they know
I' the shipman's card.
I will drain him dry as hay:
Sleep shall neither night nor day
Hang upon his pent-house lid;
He shall live a man forbid:
Weary se'nnights nine times nine
Shall he dwindle, peak and pine:
Though his bark cannot be lost,
Yet it shall be tempest-tost.
Look what I have. (1.3.2)

Macbeth
Shmoop Learning Guide

Thought: Here, the witches seem silly for conjuring a storm and casting a spell on a man whose wife refused to share some chestnuts. This pettiness seems to reflect a common problem in rural areas in the 16th and 17th centuries, where it was common for poor, old, unmarried women to be accused of witchcraft after begging for food (like chestnuts) and being turned away, especially if something bad later happened to the individuals or families that refused to help – and bad things like infertility, crop failures, illness, and unexpected deaths were *always* happening to folks back then.

This passage is also notable for the way it dramatizes a fear of women emasculating men. The First Witch not only whips up a storm to torment the sailor/husband, she also casts a spell to "drain" him or, cause him to be impotent/sterile. In the 16th and 17th centuries, some thought that witches could actually cause male impotence. Even King James (the monarch at the time the play was written) bought into this idea. Check out what he writes in the preface to *Daemonologie* (his 1603 treatise on witchcraft): "Witches can, by the power of their Master, cure or cast on diseases[...] as of weakening the nature of some men,*to make them unavailable for women.*"

BANQUO
That look not like the inhabitants o' the earth,
And yet are on't? Live you? or are you aught
That man may question? [...] You should be women,
And yet your beards forbid me to interpret
That you are so. (1.3.1)

Thought: Even Banquo is uncertain about the sisters. He wonders if they are real and whether or not they're "inhabitants" of the earth. What's interesting about this passage is the way in which Banquo's confusion about the witches ultimately registers as confusion about their *gender* – he's not sure if they're "women" because they have "beards."

Third Witch
All hail, Macbeth, thou shalt be king hereafter! (1.3.4)

Thought: The Third witch is the first to "hail" Macbeth as the future king of Scotland. The sisters' prediction certainly sets the action of the plot in motion but does that necessarily mean that they control Macbeth's actions?

BANQUO
Good sir, why do you start; and seem to fear
Things that do sound so fair? I' the name of truth,
Are ye fantastical, or that indeed
Which outwardly ye show? My noble partner
You greet with present grace and great prediction
Of noble having and of royal hope,
That he seems rapt withal: to me you speak not.

Macbeth
Shmoop Learning Guide

If you can look into the seeds of time,
And say which grain will grow and which will not,
Speak then to me, who neither beg nor fear
Your favours nor your hate. (1.3.2)

Thought: Although Banquo is confused about the weird sisters, he's also pragmatic. Macbeth, on the other hand, "seems rapt" or entranced by the witches' prophesy. Why do these two men have such different responses? Because one is more level headed than the other? Because the witches have some kind of power over Macbeth and not Banquo? Some other reason?

History Snack: Although many people (like King James) believed in and feared the power of witches, there was also plenty of skepticism about witchcraft in the 16th and 17th centuries. In 1584, Reginald Scot wrote The Discovery of Witchcraft, which set out to debunk myths about "the compacts and contracts of witches with devils and all infernal spirits or familiars [as] erroneous novelties and imaginary conceptions" (from the title page of the third edition, 1665). In *Macbeth* Shakespeare never really lands on one side or the other about the debate.

MACBETH
Into the air; and what seem'd corporal melted
As breath into the wind. Would they had stay'd!
BANQUO
Were such things here as we do speak about?
Or have we eaten on the insane root
That takes the reason prisoner? (1.3.3)

Thought: When the witches vanish into thin "air" Banquo wonders if they were ever real – "have we eaten of the insane root?" he asks. This seems like a clear indication that the witches do have supernatural powers. It also establishes a connection between the witches and several other strange visions that may or may not be real (Macbeth's hallucination of the "bloody dagger" and the appearance of Banquo's ghost, for example). Be sure to check out "Versions of Reality" for more on this.

LADY MACBETH
[…]
The raven himself is hoarse
That croaks the fatal entrance of Duncan
Under my battlements. Come, you spirits
That tend on mortal thoughts, unsex me here,
And fill me from the crown to the toe top-full
Of direst cruelty! make thick my blood;
Stop up the access and passage to remorse,
That no compunctious visitings of nature
Shake my fell purpose, nor keep peace between
The effect and it! Come to my woman's breasts,
And take my milk for gall, you murdering ministers,

**Macbeth
Shmoop Learning Guide**

*Wherever in your sightless substances
You wait on nature's mischief! Come, thick night,
And pall thee in the dunnest smoke of hell,
That my keen knife see not the wound it makes,
Nor heaven peep through the blanket of the dark,
To cry 'Hold, hold!' (1.5.3)*

Thought: We talk about this passage at length in "Quotes" for "Gender" but it's worth mentioning again here. When Lady Macbeth calls on "murdering ministers" to "unsex her" (remove her capacity to reproduce and nurture children) and fill her spirit with "direst cruelty" the play aligns her with the weird sisters, don't you think? She not only sounds like a witch (what with all the talk about spirits and "smoke of hell" but she's also acting in an "unnatural" way by stepping outside the traditional gender role prescribed for women (meek, obedient, silent, and so on). In other words, Lady Macbeth, like the "bearded" witches, is portrayed as being "too masculine."

*MACBETH
There's comfort yet; they are assailable;
Then be thou jocund: ere the bat hath flown
His cloister'd flight, ere to black Hecate's summons
The shard-borne beetle with his drowsy hums
Hath rung night's yawning peal, there shall be done
A deed of dreadful note. (3.2.4)*

Thought: Hmm. It sounds like somebody's channeling the witches. When Macbeth talks about his plans for the murder of Banquo and Fleance, he appropriates the weird sisters' language. What's that all about?

*HECATE
Have I not reason, beldams as you are,
Saucy and overbold? How did you dare
To trade and traffic with Macbeth
In riddles and affairs of death;
And I, the mistress of your charms,
The close contriver of all harms,
Was never call'd to bear my part,
Or show the glory of our art?
And, which is worse, all you have done
Hath been but for a wayward son,
Spiteful and wrathful, who, as others do,
Loves for his own ends, not for you.
(3.5.1)*

Macbeth
Shmoop Learning Guide

Thought: When Hecate (traditionally known as the goddess of witchcraft) shows up and chastises the weird sisters for taunting Macbeth without her, we're reminded that even witches have to follow orders. In a way, the witches' disobedience seems like a parallel to the way Macbeth, "the wayward son," is insubordinate to King Duncan.

But make amends now: get you gone,
And at the pit of Acheron
Meet me i' the morning: thither he
Will come to know his destiny:
Your vessels and your spells provide,
Your charms and every thing beside.
I am for the air; this night I'll spend
Unto a dismal and a fatal end:
Great business must be wrought ere noon:
Upon the corner of the moon
There hangs a vaporous drop profound;
I'll catch it ere it come to ground:
And that distill'd by magic sleights
Shall raise such artificial sprites
As by the strength of their illusion
Shall draw him on to his confusion:
He shall spurn fate, scorn death, and bear
He hopes 'bove wisdom, grace and fear:
And you all know, security
Is mortals' chiefest enemy. (3.5.1)

Thought: Hecate orders the witches to conjure "artificial sprites" (apparitions) to confuse Macbeth and instill him with a false sense of "security" that will ensure his downfall. If the witches already know Macbeth's fate, why do they bother tricking him?

ALL
Double, double toil and trouble;
Fire burn, and cauldron bubble. (4.1.1)

Thought: By now you've probably noticed that the weird sisters tend to speak in a way that sets them apart from all the other characters in the play. This passage may be their most famous utterance, by the way, and it's typical of their speech pattern. Here, each line has eight beats or, syllables. The two lines also form what's called a "rhymed couplet," which just means that it's made up of two lines that rhyme at the end (*trouble* rhymes with *bubble*). This sing-song speech has a pretty distinctive effect – it sound s a lot like a child's nursery rhyme that, for modern audiences especially, may sound silly. In the 17th century, however, many believed that witches spoke this way so it may have been terrifying for some audience to listen to. If you want to know more about the other kinds of speech in the play, check out "Writing Style."

Macbeth
Shmoop Learning Guide

Violence Quotes

DUNCAN
What bloody man is that? He can report,
As seemeth by his plight, of the revolt
The newest state. (1.2.1)

Thought: The play's second scene opens with the entrance of a "bloody man" who brings news of the battle being waged against the rebels. This image is striking (especially on stage) and it echoes throughout the entire play. The "bloody man's" appearance anticipates the image of Banquo's bloody ghost in 3.4 and the apparition of the bloody child that emerges from the witches' cauldron in 4.1.

MALCOLM
Say to the King the knowledge of the broil
As thou didst leave it.
CAPTAIN
Doubtful it stood,
As two spent swimmers that do cling together
And choke their art. (1.2.1)

Thought: When the Captain's describes the battle he uses an interesting metaphor – the opposing armies, he says, fought like two exhausted "swimmers" clinging together in such a way that made it difficult for him to tell them apart. This description lends itself to the Captain's point that, for a while, there was a lot of "doubt" about which side was winning. The fray of battle, especially hand to hand combat, is often chaotic. We could also argue that there's a sense of moral ambiguity at work here as well. Which side is in the wrong and which side is in the right? Sometimes, it's hard to say, especially when both sides are trying to kill the other.

CAPTAIN
For brave Macbeth--well he deserves that name--
Disdaining fortune, with his brandish'd steel,
Which smoked with bloody execution,
Like valour's minion carved out his passage
Till he faced the slave;
Which ne'er shook hands, nor bade farewell to him,
Till he unseam'd him from the nave to the chaps,
And fix'd his head upon our battlements.
DUNCAN
O valiant cousin! worthy gentleman! (1.2.1)

Thought: There's no doubt that Macbeth is a skilled warrior – he easily disembowels his enemy before fixing his head on a pike. It's also clear that the world of *Macbeth* is a warrior culture, where violence is deemed "valiant" and makes a man "worthy." Macbeth, in fact, is rewarded for his actions by being named Thane of Cawdor (since the previous Cawdor must be executed for

Macbeth
Shmoop Learning Guide

his treasonous behavior).

CAPTAIN
So they Doubly redoubled strokes upon the foe.
Except they meant to bathe in reeking wounds,
Or memorize another Golgotha,
I cannot tell- (1.2.2)

Thought: Here, the Captain compares the way Macbeth and Banquo redoubled their efforts against the enemy to the violence that occurred at Golgotha, where Jesus was crucified. Hmm. This is a rather odd comparison, don't you think? (Especially since Macbeth and Banquo are supposed to be war heroes and loyal defenders of King Duncan.) Shakespeare is doing a bit of foreshadowing here. Macbeth, as we know, will eventually betray and murder King Duncan.

CAPTAIN
But I am faint; my gashes cry for help.
DUNCAN
So well thy words become thee as thy wounds;
They smack of honor both. Go get him surgeons. (1.2.3)

Thought: The virtue of being injured in war is seen as particularly honorable in *Macbeth*. Notice here that when the Captain compares the flow of blood that gushes from his wounds to a voice that "cries for help," King Duncan picks up on the association between "wounds" and "words." Duncan replies that the Captain's gashes *and* his verbal report of what's been taking place on the field of battle make him an honorable man.

My thought, whose murder yet is but fantastical (1.3.9)

Thought: The play makes it clear that Macbeth's first thoughts of murdering the King are "horrible imaginings – even Macbeth is disturbed by the idea of killing Duncan. At the same time, however, it's not so surprising that Macbeth would consider killing the monarch in order to secure the crown for himself. After all, Macbeth lives in a world where violence is the norm.

LADY MACBETH
Come, you spirits
That tend on mortal thoughts, unsex me here,
And fill me from the crown to the toe top-full
Of direst cruelty! make thick my blood;
Stop up the access and passage to remorse,
That no compunctious visitings of nature
Shake my fell purpose, nor keep peace between
The effect and it! Come to my woman's breasts,
And take my milk for gall, you murdering ministers, (1.5.3)

Macbeth
Shmoop Learning Guide

Thought: Lady Macbeth calls on "murdering ministers" to "unsex" her (deprive her of her capacity to reproduce and nurture children) so that she can help her husband commit murder. Lady Macbeth assumes that being a woman and a mother will get in the way of her plans for violence. She also suggests that "direst cruelty" is synonymous with masculinity. Check out "Gender" for more on this.

MACBETH
From this moment
The very firstlings of my heart shall be
The firstlings of my hand. And even now,
To crown my thoughts with acts, be it thought and done:
The castle of Macduff I will surprise,
Seize upon Fife, give to the edge o' the sword
His wife, his babes, and all unfortunate souls
That trace him in his line. (4.1.16)

Thought: Here, Macbeth resolves to use violence in order to secure his position of power. At this point, Macbeth is completely out of control. He sees nothing wrong with killing Macduff's wife and children and is intent on wiping out Macduff's "line."

MALCOLM
Let us seek out some desolate shade and there
Weep our sad bosoms empty.
MACDUFF
Let us rather
Hold fast the mortal sword, and like good men
Bestride our downfall'n birthdom. Each new morn
New widows howl, new orphans cry, new sorrows
Strike heaven on the face, that it resounds
As if it felt with Scotland and yell'd out
Like syllable of dolor. (4.3.1)

Thought: When Malcolm suggests there's nothing to be done about Macbeth's tyranny but sit down and "weep," Macduff insists that the best thing to do is "hold fast the mortal sword" (i.e., fight). According to Macduff, being "good men" involves defending their native country (their "downfall'n birthdom"). Here, violence replaces grief for these warriors.

MALCOLM
Dispute it like a man.
MACDUFF
I shall do so,
But I must also feel it as a man.
I cannot but remember such things were
That were most precious to me. (4.3.26)

Macbeth
Shmoop Learning Guide

Thought: After Macduff learns that his family has been slaughtered, his attitude toward violence and grief seem to change slightly. Before (see 4.3.1 above), he insisted that violence should replace grief altogether. Here, however, he acknowledges that he must take the time to "feel" the loss of his family before he can take action or, "dispute" his family's death.

SIWARD
Then he is dead?
ROSS
Ay, and brought off the field: your cause of sorrow
Must not be measured by his worth, for then
It hath no end.
SIWARD
Had he his hurts before?
ROSS
Ay, on the front.
SIWARD
Why then, God's soldier be he!
Had I as many sons as I have hairs,
I would not wish them to a fairer death:
And so, his knell is knoll'd. (5.11.2)

Thought: When Siward learns that his son was killed in battle, he takes comfort in knowing that he "had his hurts before" (his wounds were on the "front" of his body), evidence that he faced his opponent head on. (If he had wounds in his back, it would have appeared that he was running away from his killer, like a "coward.") For Siward, a heroic death in battle is the best possible way for a young man to die.

Time Quotes

My noble partner
You greet with present grace and great prediction
Of noble having and of royal hope,
That he seems rapt withal: to me you speak not.
If you can look into the seeds of time,
And say which grain will grow and which will not,
Speak then to me, who neither beg nor fear
Your favours nor your hate. (1.3.2)

Thought: The witches have a relationship to the present and the future unlike any other figures in the play. After they predict that Macbeth will be named king, Banquo, using an agricultural metaphor, asks them to "look into the seeds of time" and tell him what his own future has in store.

Macbeth
Shmoop Learning Guide

[Aside] Come what come may,
Time and the hour runs through the roughest day. (1.3.11)

Thought: After hearing the witch's prophesy that he'll become king, Macbeth pushes thoughts of "murder" from his mind and says he won't lift a finger against the present king – instead, he'll leave his future to "chance." Here, Macbeth suggests he's willing to let time "run" its course and make him king. The thing is, we also notice that Macbeth speaks these lines in the kind of sing-song, rhyming voice that recalls the chanting of the weird sisters, which alerts us to the fact that Macbeth's probably *not* going to sit back and bide his time.

Thy letters have transported me beyond
This ignorant present, and I feel now
The future in the instant. (1.5.3)

Thought: When Lady Macbeth reads her husband's letter (bearing news of the witch's prophesies), her thoughts immediately turn toward the "future" that she imagines for herself and her husband. In this passage, she's says it's as though the news has "transported [her] beyond this ignorant present." Her dreams of being the wife of a king are so vivid and so real to her, it's as though time has completely collapsed. Lady Macbeth feels the "future in the *instant*."

We also want to note that her use of the term "transported" is significant because it recalls Macbeth's earlier reaction to the witch's omen. Banquo twice describes his friend as being "rapt" (1.3.2, 1.3.9). The verb "rapt" can mean "To carry away in spirit; to enrapture, *transport*" (Oxford English Dictionary). So, it's as though both Macbeth and his wife are *carried away* by the witch's prophesy.

MACBETH
My dearest love,
Duncan comes here to-night.
LADY MACBETH
And when goes hence?
MACBETH
To-morrow, as he purposes.
LADY MACBETH
O, never
Shall sun that morrow see!
Your face, my thane, is as a book where men
May read strange matters. To beguile the time,
Look like the time; bear welcome in your eye,
Your hand, your tongue: look like the innocent flower,
But be the serpent under't. He that's coming
Must be provided for: and you shall put
This night's great business into my dispatch;
Which shall to all our nights and days to come
Give solely sovereign sway and masterdom. (1.5.4)

Macbeth
Shmoop Learning Guide

Thought: Lady Macbeth makes it clear that King Duncan will not leave the Macbeths' castle alive. What's interesting about this passage is the way the couple talks about the planned murder in terms of time – "Duncan comes here *to-night*"; "*when* goes he hence"; "never / Shall sun that *morrow* see!" The pair talk about their plans as though time will come to a complete halt for King Duncan. Lady Macbeth also puns on the word "time" when she suggests Macbeth should suit his demeanor to the *occasion* ("To beguile the time, / Look like the time") in order to make Duncan believe he's happy to see him. By making sure that Duncan will never see another tomorrow, the Macbeths ensure their own future.

We might also consider what happens to the "day" when Duncan is murdered. Ross says that "by the clock, 'tis day, / And yet dark night strangles the traveling lamp" (2.4.1). When darkness falls in the middle of the day, it's as if time is completely out of joint.

If it were done when 'tis done, then 'twere well
It were done quickly: if the assassination
Could trammel up the consequence, and catch
With his surcease success; that but this blow
Might be the be-all and the end-all here,
But here, upon this bank and shoal of time,
We'l jump the life to come. (1.7.1)

Thought: Macbeth considers that even if he's not caught after he murders King Duncan, he'll be punished in the afterlife (the "life to come"). Is (temporary) earthly power worth eternal damnation?

Hang out our banners on the outward walls;
The cry is still 'They come:' our castle's strength
Will laugh a siege to scorn: here let them lie
Till famine and the ague eat them up:
Were they not forced with those that should be ours,
We might have met them dareful, beard to beard,
And beat them backward home. (5.5.1)

Thought: Macbeth's strategy during the siege is to hole up in the palace and bide his time "till famine and the augues" (starvation and illness) destroy the enemy soldiers.

MACDUFF
Boundless intemperance
In nature is a tyranny; it hath been
The untimely emptying of the happy throne
And fall of many kings.
(4.3.7)

Macbeth
Shmoop Learning Guide

Thought: Macduff's sense of King Duncan's murder is fascinating. He suggests the king's death was an "untimely" event that has had major consequences for the entire kingdom.

MACBETH
She should have died hereafter;
There would have been a time for such a word.
To-morrow, and to-morrow, and to-morrow,
Creeps in this petty pace from day to day
To the last syllable of recorded time,
And all our yesterdays have lighted fools
The way to dusty death. […] (5.5.2)

Thought: Macbeth's response to the news of his wife's death at first seems cold and callous – he doesn't have time to bother with mourning the loss because he's too busy dealing with the siege at hand. Yet, as the speech continues, it becomes clear that life has lost all meaning for Macbeth. As he utters that the words "To-morrow, and to-morrow, and to-morrow" Macbeth acknowledges, for the first time, that he has no future.

MACDUFF
Despair thy charm;
And let the angel whom thou still hast served
Tell thee, Macduff was from his mother's womb
Untimely ripp'd. (5.10.3)

Thought: When Macduff reveals that he was delivered, prematurely, via cesarean section, the witches' prophesy that Macbeth would not be harmed by any man "of woman born" makes a lot of sense. (Macduff eventually kills Macbeth.) By this time, however, it's too late for Macbeth to do anything about it.

MACDUFF
Hail, king! for so thou art: behold, where stands
The usurper's cursed head: the time is free:
I see thee compass'd with thy kingdom's pearl,
That speak my salutation in their minds;
Whose voices I desire aloud with mine:
Hail, King of Scotland! (5.11.1)

Thought: When Macduff says "the time is free" he means, in one sense, that Macbeth's reign has come to an end and the people of Scotland now live in freedom from tyranny. There's also an underlying suggestion here that time had somehow come to a halt when Macbeth murdered Duncan and became king. Now that the rightful heir, Malcolm, will be crowned monarch, linear time (which was disrupted by Macbeth), is back on track, just as lineal succession (also disrupted by Macbeth) is reestablished.

Macbeth
Shmoop Learning Guide

Plot Analysis

Classic Plot Analysis

Initial Situation
Macbeth has been mostly responsible for the crown's victory over the rebel Scots and Irish invaders. Before we even meet him, his own King and the men that fight under him have prepared us to encounter a noble, courageous, and loyal man.
In the beginning, we know where everyone stands; King Duncan is a nice old man who was going to be taken advantage of by traitors, and Macbeth, because he seems to lack mortal fear, went blazing into a losing battle and knifed a man from his navel to his neck. Heroic behavior, if ever there was any. To drive home how brave Macbeth is, there's even a second wave of rebel fighters after the whole disemboweling incident. Macbeth has no chance of winning, but wins anyway. He defeats the leader of Norway's troops by meeting him in hand-to-hand battle, "confronting him with self-comparisons." (Subtle image alert: The men are mirror images of each other in more ways than one.) Macbeth was *so* good that the Norwegian king can't even bury the dead until money is paid to Scotland. There's no moral but victory in war.

Conflict
The weird sisters prophesize that Macbeth is fated to become King of Scotland. Macbeth seems content to let it happen in due time. But then King Duncan names Malcolm as the heir to the throne and Macbeth believes he must murder the King in order to become king.
Macbeth would go home a hero, be reunited with his wife, and get back to being Thane of Glamis, except he meets some ladies on a hill who have beards and promises. Looks aside, they know just what to say to Macbeth and his traveling companion, Banquo, to stir the boys up. Macbeth is promised to be Thane of Cawdor and eventually King, and Banquo will sire heirs to the throne. Macbeth is enraptured by the power the women offer him and he reveals he has thoughts about "murder." He quickly sweeps these thoughts aside but when King Duncan says Malcolm's going to be the next king, Macbeth decides he must take action. Herein lies the conflict – no kingship unless he murders first. It also becomes clear that "fate" may not be determining Macbeth's future because Shakespeare goes out of his way to show Macbeth deliberating about what to do next. (You can read "Fate and Free Will" for more on this.) Lady Macbeth receives a letter from Macbeth about the prophecy, and resolves that Macbeth must murder Duncan, with the help of her encouragement. Macbeth takes a good look at himself, and his "if it were done when 'tis done" soliloquy reveals to him and us that nothing but blatant ambition is at the core of this act of treachery, and pure evil. What's a guy to do? Apparently it depends on what his girl says.

Complication
Macbeth kills the king to secure the kingship, but immediately it becomes clear that the only way to hide the murder is to keep murdering. Eventually murder and tyranny are the only way Macbeth can keep his power.
Thanks to Lady Macbeth's urging, Macbeth has gone ahead with the murder, and Lady Macbeth has framed the guards, but as soon as he walks out of Duncan's bedchamber with

Macbeth
Shmoop Learning Guide

bloody hands, we meet the thoughts that are to plague him. Voices cry out of the night, promising he will sleep no more since he has murdered sleep's peace. Macbeth hasn't even settled in the new palace before Macbeth has already found some local thugs to murder Banquo and his son. (Remember, the weird sisters have also prophesized that Banquo's heirs will rule the kingdom some day.) Macbeth realizes that, if Banquo's part of the prophecy comes true, he will have murdered Duncan to hand Banquo's children the crown. That's no good. Rather than rethink his whole murdering the King thing, it seems easiest to take out Banquo's son and obviously, Banquo himself. Even Lady Macbeth thinks this is a naughty idea, but Macbeth has already convinced himself it is the best course, and tells her not to think on it. In managing the affair himself, it seems he is in control, but we've already had inklings that his emotions and the conscience he represses have other ways of lashing out at him. Other *complicated* ways, that is.

Climax
The very night Macbeth is meant to celebrate his new crown, the ghost of Banquo visits him and ruins the party. Macbeth has a fit in front of all of his new subjects. It seems he isn't of sound mind to run himself, never mind the kingdom. He begins to unravel, and suspicions arise.
Macbeth is brazen, and at his dinner party, calls special attention to Banquo's absence, making it seem as though Banquo is insensitive. In fact, Banquo couldn't show up because he was dead, thanks to Macbeth. Banquo's ghost, however, shows up fashionably and climactically late – but is only seen by Macbeth. Macbeth goes into public fits of fear and anger. He complains that there was a time when the dead stayed dead – it seems he did not think his act would come back to haunt him. (Very punny.) His hysterical episode has ruined the party, and after Lady Macbeth sends everyone home, the King rants quietly to himself the prophetic fact that bloodshed only ever leads to more bloodshed.

Suspense
Macbeth visits the weird sisters to hear more of his complex fate. Where his silent conscience seemed like it was going to be his undoing, new intelligence from the sisters convinces him that he can stay King. He is drunk with power and now immune to sense. It seems good might not prevail. At the same time, forces are gathering in England to fight his tyranny.
Haunted by daggers, ghosts and nights of sleeplessness, Macbeth consults the ladies that helped him into this mess in the first place. Even his fits of madness don't deter him from pursuing his course of action. He relies on the words of the three witches like a fix, even if they seem contrary to good sense. The witches have their own evil intention of confusing the situation further. They distract Macbeth with more twisted prophecy – he walks away thinking he is invincible, ignoring the part of the prophecy that promises Banquo's sons will still be kings. In his arrogance, he has Macduff's family murdered. So Macbeth thinks he can't be killed, but we know that he must be killed if Banquo's children are to rule. In England, we find that Macduff, fiercely competent, has pledged to murder Macbeth – as soon as he can get his hands on him. Macduff's not the type to get his kilt in a knot over nothing, so we know he means business. He will bring ten thousand men and his own rage to face Macbeth. Will twisted prophecy or righteous rage win the day? Onward – to the denouement!

Denouement
The noblemen of Scotland have joined forces with the English army, and all stand together in Scotland to fight Macbeth. Lady Macbeth kills herself, and as Birnam Wood marches on

Macbeth
Shmoop Learning Guide

Dunsinane, part of the prophecy is fulfilled. Macbeth resigns himself to fate, but he's going to fight it, even though he knows it's futile. There's not much else he can do.
To the surprise of... no one, it turns out you can't trust bearded ladies' tales to help you out in any way. Macbeth hears that an army of 10,000 marches his way, but feels protected because forests don't march. This sense of security lasts right up until said forests do, in fact, start marching. In the meantime, Lady Macbeth is announced dead by her own hand, and when Macbeth hears that the woods is on its way, he resigns himself, saying he wearies of the sun. He goes out committed to dying a death full of his former soldierly violence, but perhaps not his soldierly honor.

Conclusion
The last part of the prophecy fulfilled, Macbeth stands against a man not-of-woman-born. Still he fights, but good prevails over tyranny and madness. He is slain, and Malcolm is named the rightful king.
When Macbeth comes to face Macduff, he bids him turn back. Though he killed indiscriminately before, he feels the blood of Macduff's family most heavily. Macduff also feels pretty seriously about his entire family being dead, but the time for action is upon them. Macbeth, unrepentant and clawing 'til the end, dies a bloody death befitting his bloody life. If you think you have heard these words before, in fact, yes you have, in the beginning of this full-circle play.

Booker's Seven Basic Plots Analysis: Tragedy

Anticipation Stage
Macbeth has heard the witches' prophecy that he will be King of Scotland
Before hearing this, Macbeth was pretty content with his life. Now he has horrible imaginings, ones that befit a traitor more than a war hero. Though he isn't exactly excited about murdering Duncan, he doesn't wholly dismiss the prospect.

Dream Stage
Macbeth murders Duncan and fits easily into the crown.
Macbeth frames Duncan's guards with his wife's help, casts suspicion on Duncan's sons, and takes the crown for himself. The King's sons Malcolm and Donalbain have disappeared, and no one questions Macbeth's loyalty or his guilty conscience.

Frustration Stage
The borrowed-robes-hang-loose soliloquy
With his head fresh in the crown, Macbeth feels unsafe in his newly found power until the one remaining threat is removed. Though Banquo has not cast any suspicion nor been unkind in any way, it seems best to have him (and his son Fleance) murdered – just in case. Macbeth has to ensure that he hasn't sold his soul for Banquo's gain.

Nightmare Stage
Banquo, in ghost form, comes to the banquet, held up a little by Death and looking a little pale in the face. Suspicion falls heavily on tyranny.
Banquo's ghost throws Macbeth into a public and embarrassing fit. That same night, Macbeth

Macbeth
Shmoop Learning Guide

has received intelligence that Macduff, Thane of Fife, has gone to England to gather forces with Malcolm and Siward.

Destruction stage
Macbeth visits the weird sisters. He readies for battle.
The weird sisters have given Macbeth artificial intelligence that fosters false hopes of victory in him. Macbeth's destruction lies in the fact that the prophecies come true to the rebels' advantage instead of Macbeth's. Macbeth, in a sudden burst of perception, realizes he is defeated. With his wife freshly dead and his faith sorely missed, Macbeth dies fighting. He leaves the play a warrior content with his lot – just as he entered it.

Study Questions

1. The last scene in the play, where Malcolm blesses all who have fought nobly on his side and promises to punish all who helped the traitors, is eerily reminiscent of the first scene with his father, Duncan. Is this play commenting that it's just the nature of history to repeat itself?
2. Macbeth starts the play as a hero and ends up a tyrant. Does this mean there are no truly evil people and power corrupts, or just that some people have bad judgment when choosing heroes?
3. Lady Macbeth is often hailed as the source of Macbeth's evil, but she never talks about her own gain. Even when she should be all happy as queen, she takes her own life. Is Lady Macbeth just caught in fate here? Was she just trying to do the good thing by being a supportive wife? Is good in the eye of the beholder?
4. The three witches, the weird sisters, are also often blamed for planting the seed of treachery in Macbeth's mind – yet the root of the word "wyrd" goes back to the Anglo Saxon word for "fate." Does one only need to think a thing is fate to make it happen? How much personal agency does one have against fate?
5. The good of other characters seems magnified when called out against Macbeth's evil. If not for Macbeth, Duncan would've died an aged king, Malcolm would never have tested his mettle in battle, and Macduff would've just been a good, quiet Thane of Fife, not a warrior-hero. Does it truly take the worst of times to see the best in men's natures?

Macbeth
Shmoop Learning Guide

Characters

All Characters

Macbeth Character Analysis

Macbeth is a beloved Scottish general who bravely defends his king and country in battle. After hearing the three weird sisters' prophesy that he will one day rule Scotland, Macbeth commits heinous murder and other tyrannous acts in order secure his position as king.

Macbeth and the Question of Fate
When we follow Macbeth's trajectory in the play, we're invited to consider what it is, exactly, that makes a seemingly decent man commit an "evil" act. Let's start from the beginning. When Macbeth hears the witches' prophesy, he's *very* interested in what they have to say. His thoughts also turn to "murder" (in order to fulfill said prophesy). But Macbeth is also terrified by his "horrible imaginings" – his hair stands on end and his heart races, "knock[ing] at [his] ribs." "My thought, whose murder yet is but fantastical," says Macbeth, "Shakes so my single state" (1.3.9). Macbeth *knows* that killing Duncan would be a terrible act and he's sickened by his own thoughts. So, what happens to Macbeth? What makes him kill Duncan and then order several other murders without batting an eyelash?

On the one hand, we can see Macbeth as a figure controlled by outside forces. After all, the three witches prophesize that Macbeth will become king (1.3.4) and they also know the exact circumstances of Macbeth's downfall (4.1.8), which suggests that Macbeth has no control over his own fate. What's more, the weird sisters' words clearly prompt Macbeth into action and we often get a sense that Macbeth is acting against his own will, as though he's in a trance. Think about the first time Macbeth encounters the witches – he's twice described as being "rapt" (1.3.2). Even after this encounter Macbeth, at times, seems to move through the play in a dreamlike state, as when he follows a "dagger of the mind" toward the sleeping king's room just before he commits his first murder (2.1.6). In light of this kind of evidence, it's easy to blame all of Macbeth's actions on the three witches and/or fate. (For a detailed discussion about the witches' relationship to "fate," check out our "Character Analysis" of the Weird Sisters.)

Yet, we can also argue that Macbeth has a mind of his own and acts according to his own free will. In the play, we clearly see Macbeth deliberate about murder, and then make his own choices and put his plans into action. The witches, we should point out, never say anything to Macbeth about *murdering* Duncan. When Macbeth first hears the sisters' prophesy, his thoughts turn to "murder" all on their own. (In fact, the witches never say anything at all about *how* Macbeth will become king.) So, perhaps Macbeth has had inside him a murderous ambition *all along* and the three witches merely awaken or embody a desire that's been dormant. We could argue, then, that "fate" has nothing to do with Macbeth's life at all.

Now, we don't necessarily have to be married to any of these arguments. Alternatively, we could say Macbeth is "fated" to become king but *how* he comes to the crown is entirely *up to him*. Or, we settle on the idea that Macbeth is a figure that dramatizes the ambiguity of human will and action. Why do people do the things they do, even when they know their actions are hideous? It's often a complete and utter mystery, and Shakespeare brings this point to the forefront.

Macbeth, Marriage, and Masculinity

In recent decades (that's not such a long time considering that *Macbeth* is about 400 years old), audiences have become increasingly interested in Macbeth's relationship with his wife. We have to admit that their relationship is fascinating. At the play's beginning, Macbeth treats Lady Macbeth as an equal, if not more dominant partner. In fact, when Macbeth waffles and has second thoughts about killing Duncan, it's his ambitious wife who urges him on by attacking his masculinity, a strategy that proves effective. When Macbeth says "we will proceed no further in this business," Lady Macbeth responds by asking, "Art thou afeard / To be the same in thine own act of valour / As thou art in desire?" (1.7.3-4). In other words, Lady Macbeth asks if Macbeth is worried that his performance of the act of murder will be as weak as his "desire" to kill the king.

There's also a dig at Macbeth's sexual performance at work here because Lady Macbeth implies that Macbeth is afraid his performance of killing the king will be just as weak as his performance in the bedroom (his sexual "desire"). Either way, Lady Macbeth insists her husband is acting like an impotent "coward" (1.7.3). Killing the king, like satisfying one's wife, says Lady Macbeth, will confirm Macbeth's masculinity: "When you durst *do it*, then you were a man" (1.7.4).

Macbeth, as we see, buys into this notion that "valour," however cruel, is synonymous with masculinity. "Prithee peace," he says, "I dare *do all* that may become a man" (1.7.4). Macbeth clearly associates manhood with the capacity for murder (and the ability to satisfy his wife). Perhaps this is why Macbeth assumes the dominant role in his marriage only *after* he kills Duncan. (It's also interesting that, when Macbeth plans the murder of Banquo – rejecting his wife's input in the matter altogether – he taunts his henchmen about proving *their* manhood (3.1.10). We can't help but wonder if Macbeth's ideas about what it means to be a "man" ultimately contribute to his downfall. What do you think?

Ambition

We can also read Macbeth's character as a study of ambition and its ill effects. Once Macbeth murders Duncan, he becomes willing to do *anything* necessary in order to secure his position of power. It also becomes easier and easier for Macbeth to commit heinous crimes. Without thinking twice, he orders the murders of Macduff's family, including his children. According to Macbeth, he's got to look out for his own best interests.

For mine own good
All causes shall give way. I am in blood
Stepp'd in so far that, should I wade no more,
Returning were as tedious as go o'er . (3.4.24)

By comparing his actions to wading through a bloody river, Macbeth suggests that once a man commits a murderous act for his own gain, it's impossible to stop. Turning back would be

Macbeth
Shmoop Learning Guide

"tedious." Macbeth's selfishness, acting for his "own good," ultimately makes him a hated "tyrant," which is quite a long way from being the "beloved" thane he once was. As the play progresses, Macbeth's justifications for his actions become increasingly thin and by the end, Macbeth seems like a shell of the man he once was – the entire kingdom looks forward to the day he'll be replaced by Malcolm.

Macbeth Timeline and Summary

- 1.3: Macbeth and Banquo are traveling back from the battlefield when they come upon the three witches. Macbeth is promised to be Thane of Glamis, Cawdor and eventually King. He listens, rapt, but demands to know more, and then learns from Ross that he's been made Thane of Cawdor. Macbeth justifies the morbid suggestions of the prophecy by downplaying it, saying that the prophecy is neither good nor bad. This is the first in a long line of justifications. We get the inside line that he's thinking of murdering Duncan from this scene (his first).
- 1.4: Macbeth meets with the King and other noblemen and pledges his loyalty. He iterates that everything he does is to secure the love and honor of Duncan and Duncan's children. Later, Macbeth splits for home right after Duncan announces that his own child is in the line for the crown. Macbeth would stick around to secure Malcolm's love and honor, but he has to go home to plan murdering Malcolm's father and stealing Malcolm's crown.
- 1.5: Macbeth finds a recently unsexed Lady Macbeth. He says only that Duncan is coming for a visit. After Lady Macbeth has a long speech about how she'll take care of things, he merely replies, "We will speak further."
- 1.7: Macbeth philosophizes to himself about the pros and cons of murdering the King, his cousin, whom he is sworn to protect, in his own house. He weighs eternal damnation, his obligations, Duncan's goodness, all the perks of being King and ultimately realizes he's really just acting on his own ambition. When Lady Macbeth enters, he's convinced himself that they can't go on to murder Duncan, and should instead enjoy their new titles without committing regicide. Lady Macbeth challenges his manhood, and he reveals how much he relies on her by asking, "If we should fail?" After hearing Lady Macbeth's plan, Macbeth is back on track to murdering Duncan.
- 2.1: Macbeth has a bit of a chat with Banquo, who is distressed by his dreams about the witches. Macbeth is distressed by his own plan to murder the King. While his last speech was about whether and why he should do the murder, this one focuses on the fact that he *will* do the murder, and his mind (possibly compensating for his silent conscience) has shown him the vision of a bloody dagger. He is at once resolved to kill Duncan, but a bit nervous over being found out.
- 2.2: Macbeth has murdered Duncan and seems a bit panicky. His murdering sounds woke some people up, people that cried "murder!" but then went back to sleep after saying some prayers. It stresses Macbeth out that his attempt to say "amen" stuck in his throat. He seems genuinely distressed; as he was murdering he also heard wild voices promise him he would sleep no more, as he had murdered sleep itself. He refuses to go back to the room to smear the king's guards with the king's blood and instead laments that not even the ocean could clean his hands of this deed.

- 2.3: Macbeth does a real piece of work here – he greets Macduff and Lennox who have come to wake up Duncan, treats them to some small talk and then sends Macduff to discover Duncan, whom Macbeth recently murdered. He plays the innocent and even gives a sweet speech about how with Duncan gone, grace can live no more. Also, he throws in that he killed the drunken guards in a fit of rage and love for the King, which solves the problem of them outing him for his crime.
- 3.1: Macbeth is now at his new palace, and invites Banquo to dinner after asking where he'll be that afternoon and whether or not he'll have the means to defend himself at such a time. He finds out that Banquo and his son Fleance will be horseback riding and changes the subject to gossip about Malcolm and Donalbain. He blames them for the murder, and tells Banquo they'll discuss it all later.
- After sending Banquo out, he calls in the men he has lined up to murder Banquo. He gives a little speech justifying his action, as Banquo is the only threat to him, given Banquo's disposition and knowledge. Also, the witches promised Banquo's children would be next to the throne, which doesn't look good for Macbeth's offspring. Macbeth gives a pep talk to the murderers, inventing some wrong that Banquo has done to them. Macbeth says he would kill Banquo himself, but their mutual friends wouldn't be too stoked about it. Also, he adds, Banquo's innocent son Fleance will have to be killed for good measure.
- 3.2: Macbeth conferences with Lady Macbeth, and hints that he's going to have Banquo killed. They agree to put on a good face at the dinner party, but Macbeth won't explicitly burden Lady Macbeth with the knowledge of his fifth wrongful murder. (Having killed King, guard, guard, and friend, Fleance is number five.) Macbeth appeals to the dark forces in nature to help him (or his henchmen, apparently) take action.
- 3.4: Macbeth is jovial at the dinner party, even more so when he talks with a murderer who confirms that Banquo is dead. He is unsettled to hear that Fleance is not, and then he begins having fits, seeing Banquo's ghost at the dinner table. Banquo's ghost appears twice, fittingly, each time Macbeth is making a brazen toast to Banquo who is, in Macbeth's speech, mysteriously absent. In full view of all his guests, he shouts at the invisible ghost that only he sees. Lady Macbeth sends everyone home, and Macbeth seems resigned to the fact that blood will have blood. He will visit the weird sisters tomorrow for more news.
- 4.1: Macbeth shows up on the heath to meet the witches. He compliments them on their power, but demands they answer his questions about his future. He is shown many visions and walks away with some conflicting information. He can only be defeated by a man not born of a woman, and only when Birnam forest moves to his doorstep. However, he learns the bad news that Banquo's kids, not his, will be the next line of kings. The witches disappear and Lennox finds Macbeth (who is in a rage) to tell him Macduff has fled. Macbeth will show Macduff who's boss by murdering his wife and children. He adds he will now focus on acting on his feelings immediately instead of waiting for things to go naturally.
- 5.3: Macbeth is at his castle in Dunsinane, and blusters that he needn't shake with doubt or fear because the prophecy protects him. He curses the attendant that tells him of the approach of 10,000 Englishmen, and upon confirming this news, decides to put on his armor a little early, to get ready for the battle. He asks the doctor after his wife, and hearing that she is not sick, but rather she is stricken with fantasies, demands that someone cure her. He then asks the doctor if maybe he has some way to get rid of the English army, while he's at it. Macbeth, distracted, keeps referring to the impossibility of Birnam Wood

Macbeth
Shmoop Learning Guide

marching or of men not being born of women. He seems to hope to reassure himself with repetition, which is a little device sometimes known as "denial."

- 5.5: Macbeth decides to hang banners on the castle walls, in case that somehow helps. It does not. According to Macbeth, no matter how many troops show up, Dunsinane is fortified and Macbeth's men don't need to fight – rather, they can wait in the comfort of the castle for the other forces to weary and die of hunger and fatigue and maybe boredom.
- Then news comes in that Lady Macbeth has died, and Macbeth confirms that he's not so hot on living lately, either. When he hears that the forest is marching on his castle, he resigns himself to his fate and decides to die fighting.
- 5.7: Though Birnam Wood has indeed marched on Dunsinane, Macbeth fights valiantly, repeating that he relies on the other part of the prophecy (that he can't be taken out by a naturally born man). He kills Siward's son mercilessly.
- 5.8: Macbeth faces Macduff and asks that Macduff back down, as Macbeth already feels responsible for so much of the Macduff blood being shed. Macduff won't back down, and Macbeth says he might as well fight, as he can't be beaten by anyone born by natural means (this is him repeating the prophecy yet again). Macduff lets out the spoiler that he was ripped from his mother's womb. Macbeth wishes to not fight Macduff, knowing he is bested, but his pride won't let him kneel before him, either. He fights, choosing death before his own twisted version of dishonor. He is slain and reappears as a severed head in Macduff's hands soon afterward.

Lady Macbeth Character Analysis

Lady Macbeth and her Husband
At the play's beginning, Lady Macbeth is a powerful figure: she's charming, attractive, ambitious, and seems to be completely devoted to her husband. (We might think of the pair as the original power couple.) She's also a teensy bit worried that her man isn't quite "man enough" to do what it takes to be king. According to Lady Macbeth, her husband is "too full o' the milk of human kindness" (1.5.1). If her husband's going to be the powerful figure she wants him to be, Lady Macbeth's got to take things into her own hands. Check out this famous speech where, after learning about the witches' prophesy that Macbeth will become king, Lady Macbeth psyches herself up for murder.

The raven himself is hoarse
That croaks the fatal entrance of Duncan
Under my battlements. Come, you spirits
That tend on mortal thoughts, unsex me here,
And fill me from the crown to the toe top-full
Of direst cruelty! make thick my blood;
Stop up the access and passage to remorse,
That no compunctious visitings of nature
Shake my fell purpose, nor keep peace between

Macbeth
Shmoop Learning Guide

The effect and it! Come to my woman's breasts,
And take my milk for gall, you murdering ministers,
Wherever in your sightless substances
You wait on nature's mischief! Come, thick night,
And pall thee in the dunnest smoke of hell,
That my keen knife see not the wound it makes,
Nor heaven peep through the blanket of the dark,
To cry 'Hold, hold!' (1.5.3)

It's astonishing that Lady Macbeth calls on "spirits" to aid her while she prepares to help her husband murder the king. (Shakespeare's leading ladies don't usually go around saying stuff like this. Not even Katherine Minola, who's notorious for having a tongue like a "wasp" in *Taming of the Shrew*, summons "murderous" spirits.)

First things first, though. What the heck does Lady Macbeth mean when she asks the spirits to "unsex" her? Essentially, she's asking to be stripped of everything that makes her a reproductive woman, including menstruation or, the "visitings of nature." She also asks that her breast milk be exchanged for "gall" or poison.

But why? In Lady Macbeth's mind, being a woman – especially a woman with the capacity to give birth and nurture children – interferes with her evil plans. Lady Macbeth construes femininity as compassion and kindness and also suggests that masculinity is synonymous with "direst cruelty." When Lady Macbeth says (earlier) her husband is "too full o' the milk of human kindness," she's implying that Macbeth is too much like a woman in order to wield the power necessary of a monarch (1.5.1). As we know, Lady Macbeth will use this notion of Macbeth's "kindness" against her waffling husband when she pushes him to murder the king: "When you durst do it, *then* you were a man" (1.7.4). It turns out that Lady Macbeth's attack on Macbeth's masculinity is the final nudge Macbeth needs to murder Duncan.

Witchy Woman
This makes Lady Macbeth sound pretty dangerous, kind of like the "bearded" sisters, who are also associated with an outside force that seems to push Macbeth into murderous action. In fact, Lady Macbeth's whole "unsex me" speech aligns her with witchcraft and the supernatural (calling on spirits and talking about "smoke of hell" and "murdering ministers" sure sounds witchy to us). We also want to point out that when Lady Macbeth calls on supernatural "spirits" to "fill" her with "direst cruelty," she reminds us that she also intends to "pour [her own] spirits in [Macbeth's] ear" when he returns home from battle (1.5.1). Clearly, she means to literally fill her husband's "ear" with harsh words that will help convince him to take action against Duncan but, there's also a sense that Lady Macbeth will "fill" her husband's body in the same way that women's bodies are "filled" or, impregnated by men. All of this is to say that Lady Macbeth is portrayed as masculine, and therefore, an "unnatural" figure. You can read more about the inversion of such social roles by going to "Gender."

What Happens to Lady Macbeth?
OK, sounds like Lady Macbeth is a powerful figure and may evoke some fears about dominant women. What happens to her? Soon after Macbeth proves his "manhood" by killing Duncan and becoming king, Lady Macbeth disappears into the margins of the story and becomes the kind of

weak, enfeebled figure she herself would probably despise. You want specifics? When she learns that the king's dead body has been discovered, she grows faint and must be carried from the room. (Hmm. It's almost as though Lady Macbeth has literally been drained of that "spirit" she said she was going to pour into her husband's "ear.")

Later, when Macbeth decides to murder Banquo in order to secure his position of power, he excludes his wife from the decision making altogether (3.2.5). By Act V, Lady Macbeth has been reduced to a figure who sleepwalks, continuously tries to wash the imaginary blood from her hands, and talks in her sleep of murder (5.1.1-6). She's grown so ill that the doctor says there's nothing he can do to help her. "The disease," he says, "is beyond" his "practice," and what Lady Macbeth needs is "the divine" (a priest or, God), not a "physician" (5.1.12-13).

OK, fine. So what? Well, we can read this as a kind of psychological breakdown. Lady Macbeth is so consumed by guilt for her evil acts that she eventually loses her mind. We can also say that her transformation (from a powerful and "unnaturally" masculine figure into an enfeebled woman) is significant insofar as it reestablishes a sense of "natural" gender order in the play. In other words, Lady Macbeth is put in her place as a woman – she's no longer the dominant partner in her marriage and Macbeth makes all the decisions while she sleepwalks through the palace. However we read Lady Macbeth's transformation, one thing's certain. In the end, Lady Macbeth is all but forgotten. When Macbeth learns of her death, he says he has no "time" to think about her – "She should have died hereafter; / There would have been a time for such a word" (5.5.3).

Lady Macbeth in Performance
Depending on the production, Lady Macbeth is portrayed as a virago (a brazen, war-like woman) and a manipulator, as the seed of Macbeth's evil thoughts, or as his devoted queen. (We're partial to Judy Dench's powerful and nuanced performance in Trevor Nunn's 1979 production of *Macbeth*. Watch it here.) In some productions she weeps incessantly, in some she sneers, and in some no one's really sure what she's doing. In some interpretations, she uses sexuality to convince Macbeth to do the murder the King. So, how would *you* stage Lady Macbeth?

Lady Macbeth Timeline and Summary

- 1.5: Lady Macbeth reads the letter Macbeth has sent her announcing the prophecy of the weird sisters and the greatness they promised to her husband. Lady Macbeth worries that Macbeth would like to have that greatness, but isn't strong enough to do what needs to be done to get it. Upon hearing that the King will stay with them that night, Lady Macbeth appeals to dark spirits "that tend on mortal thoughts" and asks to be the mouthpiece of their deeds. She hopes to be able to speak strongly enough to steel Macbeth to their cause. She hails Macbeth as the future king, and tells him to be strong. She'll take care of the details if he just puts a good face on it.
- 1.6: Lady Macbeth greets Duncan, his sons and the noblemen, assuring them that she is pleased to take the worries of hosting them the night. She agrees to take them to Macbeth,

Macbeth
Shmoop Learning Guide

and catches him resolving himself to not do the deed. She speaks of his manhood as being augmented by their unnatural action of murdering Duncan, and insists that if he just bounds up his courage, she has enough of a plan put together that they can pull off the murder and framing the guards. She convinces him to go through with the deed.

- 2.2: Lady Macbeth has drugged the guards and claims she is made strong by what weakens the others. She sees Macbeth, who is out of sorts after having done the deed. She is full of reassuring words, and urges him not to think so deeply of what's done, but look to the good that can be gained by it. She urges Macbeth to go wash his hands while she puts Duncan's blood on the sleeping guards. She then takes Macbeth to bed so they don't look suspicious later.
- 2.3: When alarms are sounded about Duncan's death, Lady Macbeth wakes, seemingly innocent. She mostly plays quiet, but becomes faint when she hears that Macbeth has murdered the guards, which was so not a part of the plan. She is carried from the room.
- 3.2: Lady Macbeth had earlier been with Macbeth when he was asking for Banquo's whereabouts before the big dinner party. She goes to Macbeth. He seems occupied by his own thoughts, and probes him enough to learn that he's planning something sinister. He claims Banquo's murder is all that stands between them and peace of mind. Lady Macbeth protests, as she is not so comfortable with the idea of murdering Banquo. Macbeth reassures her by saying she doesn't need to know what she doesn't need to know, but that she'll applaud him later for the courage of this act.
- 3.4: Lady Macbeth plays hostess at the Macbeths' first big dinner party as King and Queen. Her main task over the course of the night becomes stopping Macbeth from looking like a madman while he effectively acts like a madman from seeing Banquo's ghost. She tries to distract their guests, urging them to eat and ignore the King, as he is given to fits of momentary madness, but then she chides him privately for being unmanly. She tells him to chill out and then sends everyone home, as it is clear they are all disturbed by Macbeth's strange behavior. Then Macbeth seems rational again. He is ready to hatch a plan to kill the traitorous Macduff, and promises to visit the weird sisters once more. In private, she does not question his manliness again, nor does she try to reason with him, but tells him he lacks "the season of all natures, sleep." The two go to bed.
- 5.1: Next time we see Lady Macbeth, she is still sleeping, but seems weary. A doctor and gentlewoman watch her sleepwalking fit, an activity which appears to have been happening a lot lately. She comes out and reenacts bits and pieces of her own plan to murder Duncan with Macbeth, but her sleepy recounting is peppered with her own insecurities, or perhaps guilt. She cannot seem to wash the blood (or its stench) off her hands, and she cries for the wife of the Thane of Fife, perhaps knowing that Macduff, the Thane of Fife, has had his wife recently murdered by Macbeth. She hurries back to bed when she hears a knocking in her dreams, probably remembering the knocking that happened after she and Macbeth saw to Duncan's murder.
- Note: One of the Queen's most important impacts occurs offstage. She commits suicide as announced in 5.5, but we do not see her again. She is not even mourned properly by Macbeth, who at this point is driven to further violence by the same desperation that seems to have killed her.

Macbeth
Shmoop Learning Guide

Duncan Character Analysis

Duncan is the King of Scotland. While spending the night as a guest at Inverness, he's murdered by Macbeth, who has aspirations to rule the country. In the play, Duncan is a benevolent old man. We never see him out on the battlefield, and he is always full of kindly words. He's also generous when bestowing honors on the soldiers and thanes that protect him and his kingdom. Duncan is so sympathetic and likable a character that murdering him seems horrifying. His good nature, pronounced by Macbeth in his private thoughts, reminds us of what a terrible thing it is to murder him. Even Lady Macbeth, who says she would murder her own nursing babe, can't kill him because he resembles her father while sleeping. That Macbeth can murder this man exemplifies just how atrocious the act is. It's also a clear indication that Macbeth is far removed from human kindness and morality.

King Duncan's character is also interesting insofar as it speaks to the play's representation of masculinity and power. Shakespeare scholar and retired UC Berkeley professor Janet Adelman reminds us that in a world where manhood is synonymous with violence and cruelty, King Duncan is decidedly soft: "Heavily idealized, this ideally protective father is nonetheless largely ineffectual: even when he is alive, he is unable to hold his kingdom together, reliant on a series of bloody men to suppress an increasingly successful series of rebellions...For Duncan's androgyny is the object of enormous ambivalence: idealized for his nurturing paternity, he is nonetheless killed for his womanish softness, his childish trust, his inability to read men's minds in their faces, his reliance on the fighting of sons who can rebel against him" (*Suffocating Mothers: Fantasies of Maternal origin in Shakespeare's Play, Hamlet to The Tempest*).

In this way, King Duncan is a lot like the historical figure Duncane from Shakespeare's main source for the play, Volume II of Holinshed's *Chronicles of England, Scotland, and Ireland.* In *Chronicles*, Duncane is too "soft and gentle of nature" and is contrasted with Macbeth, who is "cruel of nature." Shakespeare picks up on this contrast in *Macbeth.* If, on the one hand, King Duncan is too gentle and Macbeth, on the other hand, is a tyrant when he becomes king, then is the play calling for something in between – a king that rules with authority and temperance? Check out our discussion of "Power" for more on this.

Duncan Timeline and Summary

- 1.2: We meet Duncan as he demands that a bloody Captain give him news of how the battle is going. He is full of praises for all that have fought, especially Macbeth and Banquo. He announces that Macbeth has earned the title that the Thane of Cawdor gave up by his treachery.
- 1.4: Duncan asks if Cawdor has been executed, and notes that it's impossible to figure out whom to trust, as a kind face often hides an evil mind. Duncan then meets Macbeth and Banquo, and is full of gushing praises and thanks for everyone, especially Macbeth and Banquo. He names his son the next in line to the kingship, not knowing this will only spur Macbeth to murder him.
- 1.6: Duncan arrives with his sons and noblemen to Macbeth's castle at Inverness, and is

Macbeth
Shmoop Learning Guide

full of praises for what a lovely place the castle is. At meeting Lady Macbeth, Duncan says he loves her, citing this love as the only reason he would trouble her by being her guest tonight. He professes to love Macbeth, too. This is the last we see of Duncan before his death.

Malcolm Character Analysis

Malcolm is elder son of King Duncan and newly appointed as Prince of Cumberland, known to be the holding place for the next King of Scotland. When we first meet Malcolm, he seems rather weak – he's standing around praising a brave and bloodied Captain for saving his life and rescuing him from capture. In other words, Malcolm's the kind of guy who seems to need rescuing. This doesn't exactly sound kingly, does it?

Malcolm's reaction to news of his father's death doesn't recommend him to be king yet, either; it only shows he's still feeling around for the best course of action. He seems to lack the experience to make him confident or capable. Only when he meets Macduff, who complements him in courage and experience, do we begin to see the seeds of power in Malcolm. In order to test Macduff's honor, Malcolm makes himself out to be a lecherous tyrant who's more interested in selfish gain than he is in the good of the kingdom. Everything makes sense again when Malcolm admits he's a virgin (not a letch) and was just teasing Macduff to make sure he was true to the cause of Scotland. (Note: This could be a nod to King James I of England, who was supposed to be "chaste" before he married.)

Malcolm's words at the end, praising and gifting his allies and damning his enemies, make it seem like he'll follow right in the footsteps of his dad: gracious and, for the most part, harmless. Even if Malcolm isn't going to be a tough warrior anytime soon, he has folks like Macduff to help out, so long as Malcolm can continue to make the speeches and be pure of heart, which we are sure he is.

Malcolm Timeline and Summary

- 1.1: Malcolm points out the good, bleeding Captain to his father, because if it weren't for the Captain, Malcolm would've been a captive of the Irish forces. He is full of praise for this good and bleeding man.
- 1.4: Malcolm informs his father that the Thane of Cawdor died nobly, confessing his treason and repenting it deeply. His compliment to Cawdor is backhanded, as he claims "nothing in his life became him like the leaving of it."
- 2.3: Malcolm hears of his father's death that night, and asks who has done it. Macbeth dominates the scene with his woe over their father's death, and Malcolm privately speaks to his little brother, Donalbain, about why Macbeth is giving the speeches that should be theirs. Donalbain is suspicious, and the two are too shocked yet to be grief stricken or vengeful. Malcolm says they won't tarry any longer where the murderer might still be, as

Macbeth
Shmoop Learning Guide

foul things are clearly afoot. He goes off to England and Donalbain goes to Ireland. They can tell this definitely isn't over, but safer to deal with from a distance.
- 4.3: Malcolm and Macduff are in England urging the assistance of Siward and King Edward to take arms against Macbeth, who is revealed by this time as a tyrant. Malcolm is still unsteady of Macduff's intentions, and concocts an elaborate story about how he wouldn't be a better ruler than Macbeth, because he is so lusty that he would do lots of evil things to satisfy his lust. He insists how terrible he would be, and as Macduff finally despairs, Malcolm admits that he made up all these lies to test Macduff's purpose.
- Satisfied, he commits to fighting alongside Siward with the English forces to take back Scotland. He then chats with a doctor about King Edward's ability to cure scrofula with his touch. After, Malcolm greets Ross, who has come from Scotland, and assures him they are all eager to fight Macbeth's tyranny. Malcolm, upon hearing of the murder of Macduff's family, encourages Macduff to use that rage in revenge against Macbeth. All are only more firm in their resolve.
- 5.4: Malcolm hatches the plan to cover all the soldiers with boughs to hide their numbers. He announces that they should have hope, as even the men that fight alongside Macbeth do not believe in his cause.
- 5.6: Malcolm leads the charge for the soldiers to throw off their trees and begin the fight. Siward and his son will lead the battle, and Macduff and Malcolm will take care of the rest.
- 5.9: Malcolm misses the friends that have not yet returned from the fray of battle, and hearing that his cousin young Siward is dead, promises he will graciously mourn him his whole worth, taking up where his uncle leaves off. After Macduff returns with Macbeth's head, Malcolm is hailed as King. He declares a new age will be ushered in, where the valiant warriors will be rewarded for their service, and those who helped Macbeth will be called to account. He names all the Scottish thanes as earls, an English title that is new to their country. He promises all other matters that will settle the country to normalcy will come soon, and invites everyone to his coronation at Scone.

Banquo Character Analysis

Banquo is a general in the King's army (same as Macbeth) and is often seen in contrast to Macbeth. Banquo is the only one with Macbeth when he hears the first prophecy of the weird sisters; during the same prophecy, Banquo is told that his children will be kings, though he will not be. How Macbeth plays his part of the prophecy to be fulfilled makes the play – how Banquo does *not* creates a nice contrast to our main character.

From the very first time we meet Banquo, he sets himself apart from Macbeth, especially notable because both characters are introduced into the play at the same time: their meeting with the witches. While Macbeth is eager to jump all over the weird sisters' words, Banquo displays a caution and wisdom contrary to Macbeth's puppy-dog excitement. He notes that evil tends to beget evil. Though, we might want to keep in mind that in Banquo's last private speech, when he knows Macbeth has done wrong, he still thinks of what good might be coming to *him* as a result of the prophecy.

Macbeth
Shmoop Learning Guide

It's also important to note that King James I of England (a.k.a. King James VI of Scotland), the guy who was monarch when Shakespeare wrote *Macbeth*, traced his lineage back to Banquo so it's important that Shakespeare portrays Banquo as a noble figure. (In Shakespeare's source for the play, Holinshed's *Chronicles*, Banquo helps Macbeth kill the king.) We talk about this more in "Power" so be sure to check out "Quotes."

Banquo Timeline and Summary

- 1.3: Banquo is the first to notice the three weird sisters on the ride back from battle with Macbeth. He wonders at their natures, sensing something is foul by the fact that they seem to inhabit the earth, yet they don't look as things of the earth. When the witches hail Macbeth with his accursed good news, Banquo comments what they say seems nice, and he wonders why Macbeth looks so afraid.
- Rather than be afraid himself, he asks the women to look into his future, to say whether it is good or bad. They tell him that he'll bear a line of kings, though he won't be one, and he will at once be greater and lesser than Macbeth, and happier and less happy than Macbeth.
- The witches disappear, and Banquo wonders whether he and Macbeth have eaten "the insane root" since they have seen such fantastical things as these women.
- When Ross enters announcing that Macbeth is now Thane of Cawdor (just as the witches prophesied), Banquo asks if the Devil can speak true.
- While Macbeth is already hatching his nasty plan, Banquo is cautious. He notes that the deepest consequences can come from trifling with evil, which would tell you nice things in order to bring you over to the dark side. Banquo notices Macbeth is distracted, and agrees to speak with him on it later.
- 1.4: Banquo is greeted by Duncan as Macbeth is, and though he is given no specific honor, he is told that he is close to the King's own heart. Banquo humbly insists that any seed of greatness that the King plants in Banquo is the King's to reap.
- 1.6: Banquo goes to Inverness (Macbeth's home) with the King and company. Here, he gives a pretty speech about the home of the martin, judging that if that wonderful bird should make its cradle there, the air must be soft and good. (Banquo, it might be said, is not so astute about how to protect one's family and one's self.)
- 2.1: Banquo and his son Fleance are up late at Macbeth's house. Banquo can't sleep because he is plagued by "cursed thoughts" that he says nature brings to him in sleep. He meets Macbeth walking in the hall, and tells him he dreamt of the weird sisters, which Macbeth brushes off. Cryptically, Macbeth tells Banquo if he will support his cause, it would be an honor to Banquo. Banquo replies that his allegiance is clear (implicitly an allegiance to good and to Duncan) and the two again agree to talk more later.
- 2.3: Banquo wakes with all the others upon hearing of the King's murder, and is horrified. While Macbeth is busy making long talk, it is Macduff and Banquo who attend to his wife, who has grown faint on hearing about Macbeth's murder of the guards.
- 3.1: Banquo already suspects Macbeth of some wrongdoing, as the prophecy has come true but in a most awful way. Instead of ruminating on this, Banquo asks whether his part of the prophecy, that he would sire kings, might come true, too. There is no moral tongue

wagging here, as Banquo is interrupted by Macbeth and Lady Macbeth, who invite him to dinner after inquiring where he will be at a certain hour of the day. He, innocent of any bad intentions on their part, tells them he will be on a horseback ride with his son Fleance, but will be glad to attend dinner with them later.
- 3.3: Banquo returns to Forres and is about to attend the big dinner when he is accosted by the murderers Macbeth sent. He says it looks like rain, and the murderers have at him. At his dying breath, he denounces what he knows to be Macbeth's treachery, and bids his fleeing son to avenge his honor.
- Note: Banquo's ghost is written into the following banquet scene, and is shown in some productions, while others keep it in the mind's eye of a guilty Macbeth. The ghost does not speak, but gets his haunting on quite effectively anyway.

Macduff Character Analysis

Macduff is a loyal Scottish nobleman and the Thane of Fife. After Macbeth murders Macduff's family, Macduff grieves for his loved ones and then resolves to kill Macbeth in man-to-man combat. At the play's end, he triumphantly carries Macbeth's severed head to Malcolm, the future king.

Macduff is not a man of many words, but he is one of the few characters in the play whose absence or silence speaks as much for him as his words. When Macduff speaks, you listen, because it's a rarity and because it's generally sensible and genuine. We first hear Macduff as he expresses honest grief at the King's murder, which he discovered. As we get to know Macduff, who is a strong and courageous soldier, we can appreciate how awful and deeply he felt Duncan's murder. It takes a lot to make this kind of man ramble on about his feelings. Macduff is additionally sharp and attentive; while everyone else panics and dithers about Duncan's death, Macduff is the one that asks why Macbeth killed the guards senselessly. He is also the first to see to the ailing Lady Macbeth, who cries for help upon hearing the news about the guards. Everyone else is too wrapped up in Macbeth's passion to do the practical thing and help the Lady. (Though, we should also note that Macduff mistakenly assumes that because Lady Macbeth is a woman, she's a fragile flower. He has no idea she played a big role in Duncan's death)

As the play unfolds, Macduff speaks with Ross about what's up, and there's no long "woe-be-unto man and Scotland" speeches. Instead of prattling on about his suspicions of the King, Macduff makes the quiet and powerful decision to just leave for England. This is not a cowardly act, but rather a brave one intended to aid Malcolm (who needs all the help he can get) in enlisting the English against Macbeth. It is clear from his talk with Malcolm that Macduff loves Scotland and is not willing to see her maligned by a new boss.

We truly discover the strength of Macduff's character when he meets with Ross and receives the terrible news of his family's murder. When Macduff hears of his loved ones' deaths, he is not afraid to express emotion and to grieve openly for his loss, despite Malcolm's insistence that he needs to be a "man" and get busy killing the guy responsible for his loss. This is a huge

Macbeth
Shmoop Learning Guide

deal because Macduff is the *only* person in the play who insists that being a "man" means being able to "feel" things. Everybody else in *Macbeth* runs around insisting that masculinity is synonymous with violence and even cruelty. Not so, according to Macduff. Real men are able to express emotion.

Macduff Timeline and Summary

- 1.6: Macduff first enters the play when the King and noblemen arrive at Inverness to stay with Macbeth. He has no lines in the scene, which is noteworthy only because the scene is filled with the fawning of his fellows. While they go on and on about how wonderful Macbeth's castle is, Macduff is silent.
- 2.3: Macduff arrives with Lennox to wake the King, and is the one to discover that Duncan has been murdered. He calls it for the horror that it is, no flip-flopping or abstraction like Banquo, Macbeth and Lady Macbeth are prone to. He notes that the King is the Lord's anointed temple, indicating he believes that Kings receive their power directly from God. When Lady Macbeth enters with questions, he gently defers telling her the truth, suggesting that her woman's nature is too gentle to bear it. Irony at its best. Macduff cries out to Banquo about what has happened and is clearly stricken with honest grief. As Macbeth makes his speeches about Duncan, Macduff is the one to note his casual line about murdering the guards. He asks why Macbeth would do so; Macbeth prattles on. Macduff is the first to notice that Lady Macbeth is faint at Macbeth's news, and asks someone to tend to her.
- 2.4: Macduff speaks with Ross and conveys the news that the murderers are dead, slain by Macbeth, and notes that Malcolm and Donalbain have put suspicion on themselves by fleeing. He also informs Ross that Macbeth is thus named the new King. Interestingly, he will go home to Fife and his family instead of going to see the coronation.
- 4.3: Macduff is in England with Malcolm. We learned earlier that Macbeth had sent for Macduff's aid when he learned that Malcolm meant to gather rebellious forces. Macduff sent a clear "no" back to Macbeth, making his allegiance to Malcolm and his suspicion of Macbeth certain. Malcolm suggests they weep over the state of Scotland, and Macduff comforts him like a father. Macduff says it would be more fitting to take up arms to protect their homeland than to weep over her. Then comes Malcolm's speech where he tests Macduff's honesty to the cause of Scotland. After Malcolm paints a terrible picture of the letch he is, Macduff doesn't pretend to be OK with it. He says Malcolm is not only unfit to govern, but unfit to live if what he says is true. Malcolm admits he was lying, and Macduff replies simply that "such welcome and unwelcome things at once" are hard to reconcile.
- Ross meets Macduff and Malcolm, and Macduff immediately asks after his family. When Ross admits he has bad news (about ten minutes after saying they are well), Macduff demands to hear it fast. Ross says Macduff's wife and children are murdered, and Macduff, shocked, asks him to repeat the terrible news. He blames himself for their deaths, as it seems they took the ill consequence of his leaving. Malcolm encourages him to use these feelings to storm up revenge. Macduff then gives no pretty speeches, but pledges to fight Macbeth himself.
- 5.4: Macduff enters Birnam Wood with other noblemen and the army. The others plan and

Macbeth
Shmoop Learning Guide

discuss what's going on at Macbeth's house, but Macduff is mostly silent. He only cautions that they should focus on the battle and await its true outcome before thinking they have won.
- 5.7: Macduff runs around the battle seeking Macbeth. He says his family's ghosts will haunt him if Macbeth is killed by any other. He will not fight any of Macbeth's footmen or their flag bearers, but wishes to kill Macbeth only. He exits with "Let me find him, Fortune! And more I beg not."
- 5.8: Macbeth and Macduff meet on the battlefield. Macbeth asks Macduff to turn back, as he is already charged with too much of Macduff's blood. Macduff counters that he has no words, that his sword should be his voice. He then laughs at Macbeth's protective prophecy, as he seems fated to kill Macbeth, since he was not of woman-born, but rather torn from his mother's womb. He does brighten up when detailing to Macbeth how they'll impale his head on a pole for being such an un-fun tyrant. Macduff says no more, and slays Macbeth.
- 5.9: Macduff arrives with Macbeth's head and pronounces Malcolm the rightful king. He imagines that the good crowd surrounding Malcolm shares his good thoughts. Macduff sums up his feelings with a short and sweet, "Hail, King of Scotland!" to Malcolm. You can imagine this is more than the paltry fawning of lesser men, as Macduff cries it out while brandishing the gory head of the former King of Scotland.

Weird Sisters (the Witches) Character Analysis

The three weird sisters set the action of the play in motion when they confront Macbeth and prophesize that he will be King of Scotland. We never see them apart and they often speak and act in unison so it's worth considering them here as a single unit.

Ambiguity

From the play's beginnings, lots of ambiguity and drama surrounds these figures. When we encounter them in the play's opening scene, we're not sure where they've come from, who/what they are, or what they have in mind when they say they plan to meet Macbeth. What we do know is that they've gathered amidst thunder and lightening and move about the fog and "filthy" air, which seems just as murky and mysterious as they are. Even Banquo and Macbeth are unsure about the sisters' identity when they meet them on the heath.

> *[…] What are these*
> *So wither'd and so wild in their attire,*
> *That look not like the inhabitants o' the earth,*
> *And yet are on't? Live you? or are you aught*
> *That man may question? (1.3.1)*

Appropriately, the weird sisters deliver the infamous lines that set the tone for the play: "Fair is foul and foul is fair" (1.1.4). In other words, nothing, including the identity of the weird sisters, is certain in this play.

Macbeth
Shmoop Learning Guide

Witchcraft
The play's subheadings and stage directions refer to the sisters as "witches," which makes a lot sense, given that they spend most of their time gathered around a bubbling cauldron, chanting, casting spells, conjuring visions of the future, and goading Macbeth into murder by making accurate predictions of the future (before they vanish into thin air, of course). The witches also do some interesting things with "Eye of newt and toe of frog, / Wool of bat and tongue of dog" (4.1.2). Do you notice the sing-song quality of the speech? The sisters' chanting sounds a lot like a scary nursery rhyme, which, depending on the attitude of the audience, can have the effect of making them sound a bit silly, despite their malevolent intentions. (See "Writing Style" for a discussion of how the sisters' speech sets them apart from other characters in the play.)

While the witches can, at times, seem harmless and even a bit petty (as when they cast a spell on a man after his wife refuses to share her chestnuts with one of them), they're often portrayed as evil forces with very real powers. You can read more about them by going to the theme of "Supernatural."

The Sisters and Fate
The sisters are called "witches" only once in the play, as opposed to being referred to as "weird" a total of six times. The term "weird," as we know, comes from the Old English term "wyrd," meaning "fate" so it seems pretty clear that they're in some way associated with the three fates of classical mythology. Why does this matter? Well, the "fates" are supposed to control man's destiny and one of the major questions in the play revolves around the issue of whether or not Macbeth's actions are governed by his own free will or by some outside force. It's possible that the weird sisters control Macbeth's actions and cause him to commit murder. On the other hand, it could be that they merely set things in motion and/or represent Macbeth's murderous ambition, which you can read more about by checking out "Quotes" for "Fate and Free Will."

Character Roles

Protagonist
Macbeth
The action of the play revolves entirely around Macbeth. Usually, the protagonist is something of the play's hero, but in *Macbeth* the protagonist is more of a cautionary tale. At first, Macbeth is considered a war hero and a loyal subject to King Duncan. After the weird sisters reveal a prophesy that Macbeth will reign as king, our protagonist's ambition gets the better of him and carries out evil acts in order to secure his position of power until, finally, Macbeth meets his tragic end.

Guide/Mentor
The Three Witches
The weird sisters and Lady Macbeth are often thought of as egging Macbeth on towards fulfilling his evil thoughts. Until he meets the witches, we've only heard of him as a hero, but after his meeting, he's already telling us about his horrible "imaginings" to murder the King. Agents of darkness themselves, the witches can be seen as leading Macbeth down the path of

Macbeth
Shmoop Learning Guide

evil. It's important to note here that when Hecate, goddess of the witches, chides the sisters for acting without her, she says Macbeth has his own ends, not theirs, in mind. Things like this indicate that maybe Macbeth only needed a crutch to act on what was already brewing in his twisted mind.

Guide/Mentor
Lady Macbeth
Lady Macbeth's influence as a guide in Macbeth's life is clearer than that of the witches: when Macbeth does some ruminating on killing Duncan and decides, "We'll go no further in this business," the Lady convinces him in about 50 lines that the King must be killed. Macbeth appears to borrow Lady Macbeth's "undaunted mettle" to get the courage to go through with the murder of Duncan. Like any mentor or guide, Lady Macbeth can only go with him so far before she stops being useful. Macbeth's first murder is definitely accomplished with her aid, but as he gains experience, he becomes so hardened to cruel acts that her aid is unneeded. Once Macbeth is established as a tyrannical character without remorse, not even her death can shake him.

Foil
Banquo to Macbeth
Macbeth has many foils because he plays many roles in the play. Banquo is introduced with Macbeth, and shares his rank as one of the King's generals. Though Banquo is promised glory by the witches, he is immediately aware that they work for the Devil and their work, therefore, can't be any good. Rather than become obsessed with their prophetic promise, he thinks on it quietly and does nothing about it. It's important to note here that Banquo, up to his death, is always *promising* to discuss their meeting with the witches with Macbeth – later, when they both have time. While Banquo is thinking on it and always bringing it up, Macbeth is ignoring thought and instead acting on it. Even as he plots to kill Banquo, Macbeth notes that Banquo's noble nature is a rebuke to Macbeth's own (murdering) genius.

History Snack: In Holinshed's *Chronicles* (a major source text for the play) Banquo helps Macbeth murder the King. It seems important for Shakespeare to leave his Banquo untainted by the King's blood since King James I of England (a.k.a. King James VI of Scotland) traced his lineage back to the historical Banquo. (James sat on the throne when *Macbeth* was written.)

Foil
Duncan and Macduff as similar foils to Macbeth
Duncan and Macduff represent the noblest aspects of what Macbeth is not; Duncan is a kindly and compassionate ruler, while Macbeth is clearly more consumed with his own powers than the affairs of state. Macduff, unlike Macbeth, does not act rashly. Where Macbeth is inspired by suggestion, Macduff only acts in response to action. His family is murdered, so he takes revenge, which is decidedly different than Macbeth merely hearing that Macduff has fled, assuming he is a traitor, and having Macduff's family killed.

Foil
Lady Macduff to Lady Macbeth
Lady Macduff can be seen as a mirror image to Lady Macbeth – she is willing to chastise her husband for his unkind act of leaving, whereas Lady Macbeth doesn't ever meaningfully speak

Macbeth
Shmoop Learning Guide

with her husband once his actions get out of hand. Lady Macbeth claims that she'd be willing to murder her own children if the need arose. This is a contrast to the domestic picture of Lady Macduff playfully teasing with her own child at home.

Character Clues

Actions
One of the central divisions in Macbeth is between those who talk about acting, and those who act. Banquo's aside shows him to be more of a thinker than actor, and Macbeth's growth towards being a full-blown tyrant can be mapped by how often he talks and thinks about what he's about to do. It takes many scenes of thought and talk for Macbeth to kill Duncan, but later, he decides to off Macduff's whole family in one fell swoop because Macduff's name is mentioned. For Macbeth, thought often inhibits action, and if action is a sign of manliness and power, it's something he can always use a little more of.

Family Life
Domestic life is revealing in this play. Lady Macbeth tends to control her husband's actions at the play's beginning. She not only chastises him for not acting like a "man," she also goads him into murdering King Duncan when he waffles (1.7.3). Lady Macbeth also has a striking relationship to motherhood. She calls on spirits to "unsex" her (1.5.1) and claims that even though she knows what it's like to breastfeed, she wouldn't hesitate to tear a child from her breast and bash its brains in *if* she had promised her husband she would do it (1.7.4). Lady Macduff, on the other hand, is portrayed as a loving and doting mother. Even after her husband deserts the family she banters good-naturedly with her young son (4.2.3).

Physical Appearances
Although the play goes out of its way to show that appearances can be deceptive (check out "Versions of Reality" for more on this), there are a few key moments where characters' physical appearances help define them. The weird sisters are notable because they're bearded (1.3.1) which is a marker of their ambiguous nature and gender. They're not only mysterious but they also invert traditional gender roles assigned to women (meek, silent, obedient, kind) by casting spells and steering Macbeth toward destruction. At various moments in the play, a man's battle wounds are markers of honor and valor. King Duncan insists that the bloody Captain's gashes "speak" volumes about his heroic deeds (1.2.4) and Young Siward is deemed a "man" when his corpse is discovered to have wounds on the front of his body, a sign that he was not killed while running away (5.11.4).

Literary Devices

Symbols, Imagery, Allegory

Light and Darkness
Macbeth is full of imagery of light and darkness. From the first, the cover of night is invoked

Macbeth
Shmoop Learning Guide

whenever anything terrible is going to happen. Lady Macbeth, for example, asks "thick night" to come with the "smoke of hell," so her knife might not see the wound it makes in the peacefully sleeping King (1.5.3). The literal darkness Lady Macbeth calls for seems to correspond to the evil or "dark" act she plans to commit.

When Lady Macbeth calls for the murderous spirits to prevent "heaven" from "peep[ing] through the blanket of the dark to cry 'Hold, Hold!'" she implies that light (here associated with God, heaven, and goodness) offers protection from evil and is the only thing that could stop her from murdering Duncan (1.5.3). So, it's no surprise to us that, when Lady Macbeth descends into madness, she insists on always having a candle or, "light" about her (5.1.4) as if the light might protect her against the evil forces she herself summonsed in Act I, scene v. It turns out, though, that such candlelight doesn't do her much good – she's too far gone and ultimately kills herself.

Interestingly enough, Macbeth responds to the news of Lady Macbeth's suicide by proclaiming "out, out brief candle" (5.5.3). By now, the candle's flame has become a metaphor for her short life and sudden death. Similarly, Banquo's torchlight (the one that illuminates him just enough so his murderers can see what they're doing) is also *snuffed out* the moment he's killed (3.3.5). Both incidents recall an event from the evening King Duncan is murdered – Lennox reports that the fire in his chimney was mysteriously "blown" out (2.3.3).

Nature in Turmoil and Rebellion

After King Duncan is murdered by Macbeth, we learn from the Old Man and Ross that some strange and "unnatural" things have been going on. Even though it's the middle of the day, the "dark night strangles the traveling lamp," which literally means that darkness fills the sky and chokes out the sun (2.4.1). Could this be another allusion to the way the king's life has been extinguished (kings are often associated with the sun's power) and his power usurped by "darkness" (Macbeth)? This interpretation seems likely.

We also learn that an owl was seen killing a falcon and Duncan's horses went wild and began eating each other (2.4.2-5). Let's think about this. Clearly, nature is out of whack. Owls are supposed to prey on mice – not go around eating larger birds of prey like falcons. And Duncan's horses? Once tame, they "broke their stalls […] contending 'gainst obedience" just before they ate each other (2.4.5). Hmm. We're detecting a theme of rebellion here. It seems as though Macbeth has upset the natural order of things by killing the king.

We also want to note that the play begins with a terrible storm (likely conjured by the witches) that's associated with dark forces and also the rebellion against King Duncan.

FIRST WITCH
When shall we three meet again
In thunder, lightning, or in rain?
SECOND WITCH
When the hurlyburly's done,
When the battle's lost and won. (1.1.1)

The word "hurlyburly" means "tumult" and can apply to either or both the literal storm and "the

Macbeth
Shmoop Learning Guide

battle" that's being waged between the king's forces and the rebels (led by the traitorous Macdonwald and Cawdor).

Eight Kings

When Macbeth visits the weird sisters and demands to know whether or not Banquo's heirs will become kings, the witches conjure a vision of eight kings, the last of which holds a mirror that reflects on many more such kings (4.8.1). The fact that these are Banquo's heirs makes Macbeth really unhappy. It's important to note that one of the kings in the mirror happens to be holding two orbs and is a symbolic representation of King James I of England (a.k.a. King James VI of Scotland), who traced his lineage back to Banquo. At James's coronation ceremony in England (1603), James held two orbs (one representing England and one representing Scotland). We can't forget that King James was a major patron of Shakespeare, and that the Bard here shows his debt of gratitude to the King by exploring James's Scottish roots and confirming the lineage of an *English* king.

The "Equivocator" at the gate

The drunken Porter responds to the knocking at the castle's gates just after Macbeth has murdered King Duncan. As he does so, he imagines there's a Catholic "equivocator" at the door "who committed treason enough for God's sake" (2.3.1). This is almost certainly a reference to Jesuit Henry Garnet, a man who was tried and executed for his role in the Gunpowder Plot of 1605 (an unsuccessful attempt by a group of Catholic extremists to blow up Parliament and King James I with a keg of gunpowder). Henry Garnet wrote the "Treatise on Equivocation," which encouraged Catholics to speak ambiguously or, "equivocate" when they were being questioned by Protestant inquisitors (so they wouldn't be persecuted for their religious beliefs). This is exactly what Garnet did when he stood trial for treason.

Equivocation (speaking ambiguously or not telling the whole truth) resurfaces throughout the play. The witches tell partial truths when they make predictions, Macbeth frequently bends the truth as he deliberates about whether or not it's OK to murder the king, and Macbeth also equivocates when he justifies (to his henchmen) that murdering Banquo is acceptable.

Bloody Daggers and Hands

Blood shows up *a lot* in this play. Blood as a result of actual wounds is almost omnipresent, from the bleeding Captain in the beginning to Macbeth's bleeding head at the end. But it's the *imagined* blood that arguably has the biggest impact as a symbol. When Macbeth considers murdering Duncan, he sees a floating "dagger of the mind" that points him in the direction of the sleeping king's room (2.1.6). As Macbeth wonders if his mind is playing tricks on him, the dagger becomes covered in imaginary blood, which anticipates the way that *very real* daggers will be soiled when Macbeth murders King Duncan.

Still, it's not clear where the image comes from. Did the witches conjure it up? Is it a product of Macbeth's imagination? Is Macbeth being tempted to follow or warned not to pursue the hallucination? Eventually, imagined blood comes to symbolize guilt for both Macbeth and Lady Macbeth. After he murders Duncan, Macbeth supposes that even "Great Neptune's ocean" could not wash away his stain of guilt (2.2.13). This, of course, is in response to Lady Macbeth's command that Macbeth "go get some water / And wash this filthy witness" from his hands (2.2.10). The idea that water alone could cleanse the pair after such a foul deed seems

Macbeth
Shmoop Learning Guide

laughable, especially when Lady Macbeth famously curses the imaginary "spot" of blood she can't seem to wash from her guilty hands (5.1.1). After Macbeth kills his friend Banquo, who returns as a ghost, Macbeth announces that blood will beget blood, and his image of wading in a river of blood sums up the lesson: once you've gone far enough in spilling it, you might just as well keep on going (3.4.24).

Dead Children

You may have noticed the play is full of dead babies and slain children. The witches throw into their cauldron a "finger of birth-strangled babe" and then conjure an apparition of a bloody child that says Macbeth will not be harmed by any man "of woman born" (4.1.2). Also, Fleance witnesses his father's murder before nearly being killed himself ; Macbeth kills Young Siward; and Macduff's young son, his "pretty chicken," is called an "egg" before he's murdered. So, what's the deal?

If we think about it, the play seems fixated on what happens when family lines are extinguished, which is exactly what Macbeth has in mind when he orders the murders of his enemies' children. His willingness to kill kids, by the way, is a clear sign that he's passed the point of no return. We can trace all of this back to Macbeth's anger that Banquo's "children shall be kings" (1.3.5) and Macbeth's will not. Recall the way he laments that, when the witches predicted he would be king, they placed a "fruitless crown" upon his head and a "barren scepter" in his hands (3.1.8).

Of course, when Macbeth kills Duncan and takes the crown, Malcolm (King Duncan's heir) is denied "the due of birth." There's a sense of major political and lineal disorder here (3.6.1). By the play's end, order is restored with the promise of Malcolm being crowned as rightful king. And, we also know that Banquo's line will rule for generations to come. So, it's rather fitting that, in the end, Macbeth is killed by a man who was "untimely ripped" from his mother's womb, don't you think? (That would be Macduff, who turns out to be the guy who is not "of woman born." He was delivered via cesarean section, which doesn't count as being "born" in this play.)

Clothing

Clothing shows up an awful lot in the play – it seems like there's always talk about robes and nightgowns and what not. Was there a sale at Old Navy or is something else going on here?

Let's think about this for a minute. When Macbeth first hears that he's been named the Thane of Cawdor, he asks Angus why he is being dressed in "borrowed" robes (1.3.7). Macbeth doesn't *literally* mean that he's going to wear the old thane's hand-me-down clothing. Here, "robes" is a metaphor for the title (Thane of Cawdor) that Macbeth doesn't think belongs to him. (At this point in the play, Macbeth is corrupt.) OK. Seems like clothing metaphors are going to be about power in *Macbeth*, right?

Toward the end of the play (when everybody hates Macbeth, who has become a corrupt monarch), Angus says that Macbeth's kingly "title" is ill-fitting and hangs on him rather loosely, "like a giant's robe / Upon a dwarfish thief" (5.2.2). Angus isn't accusing Macbeth of stealing and wearing the old king's favorite jacket, he's accusing Macbeth of stealing the king's *power* (by killing him) and then parading around with the king's title, which doesn't seem to suit him at all. We can use our own clothing metaphor to say that Macbeth's not quite "big enough" to fill the former king's shoes.

There are other some ways to read the clothing metaphor. In a famous book called *The Well-Wrought Urn*, literary critic Cleanth Brooks offers a lengthy discussion about the play's clothing imagery. Here's what he has to say about Angus's comment that Macbeth looks like a "dwarfish thief" wearing a "giant's robe":

The crucial point of the comparison, it seems to me, lies not in the smallness of the man and the largeness of the robes, but rather in the fact that—whether the man be large or small—these are not his garments; in Macbeth's case they are actually stolen garments. Macbeth is uncomfortable in them because he is continually conscious of the fact that they do not belong to him. There is a further point, and it is one of the utmost importance; the oldest symbol for the hypocrite is that of a man who cloaks his true nature under a disguise. (48)

Brooks's point is slightly different than our own. He believes that the point of all this is not necessarily that Macbeth can't fill the king's big shoes, so to speak, but that Macbeth looks "uncomfortable" as king because he's stolen the crown from Duncan and he knows it doesn't belong to him. Brooks also argues that the clothing metaphor is about deception and hypocrisy, which, as we know, runs throughout the play.

There's a lot to say about Macbeth's "robes" so we'll want to keep an eye on this as we read the play.

Setting

Scotland and England in the 11th century

The play opens on a foggy heath amidst a terrible thunder storm. Most of the subsequent action also takes place under the cover of darkness, whether it's at Macbeth's first castle, Inverness, or later, at the palace in Dunsinane. Despite these set changes, the staging of the play can be done very sparsely. Minimal furniture, excessive darkness, and thunderous sound effects add to the already eerie atmosphere. Light and shadow are so central to the play that they might be considered their own set-piece as well.

Macbeth is the only Shakespearean play that's set in Scotland. (This likely has something to do with the fact that after Queen Elizabeth I died in 1603, and King James VI of Scotland was crowned King James I of England, just a few years before the play was written. FYI: James also dubbed Shakespeare's acting company "The King's Men" so, Shakespeare may have been aiming to please the monarch.) Though the play is set in the 11th century, there are plenty of allusions to contemporary (that is, 17th century) events that would have resonated with Shakespeare's original audience. There's an allusion to the Gunpowder Plot of 1605 in Act II, Scene iii and the play portrays King James I in the witches' apparition in Act iv, Scene i. Check out "Quotes" for "Power" for more on this.

Genre

Tragedy

People are always running around saying that *Macbeth* is one of the "greatest tragedies ever written." This might be true, but what the heck's a "tragedy" anyway? (We need to know the answer to this before we can even think about whether or not it's "one of the greatest," right?) It turns out there are some basic rules and conventions that govern the genre of "tragedy" so let's take a peek at our handy-dandy checklist so that we can all be on the same page.

Dramatic work: Check. *Macbeth's* a play, that's for sure.

Serious or somber theme: The play's all about what causes people to commit evil acts (like murder). So, check.

Hero's got a major flaw of character or conflict with some overpowering force: Check. Macbeth's got some serious ambition (so does his wife), which makes him willing to kill in order to secure his position as King of Scotland. Plus, once Macbeth eliminates Duncan, he can't seem to stop killing people. Is there some other "overpowering force" at work too? Keep reading.

Hero is destined for destruction and downfall: Here's where Shakespeare mixes things up. On the one hand, the "weird sisters" (three witches) prophesize that Macbeth will become King of Scotland. As we know, "weird" comes from the old English ("wyrd") word for "fate," which aligns the witches with the three fates, who are supposed to control man's destiny. So, does that mean the witches control Macbeth's fate? If the answer to this question is yes, then Macbeth is *destined* to murder Duncan, become king, and get then later get his own head lopped off by his disgruntled countryman. But this isn't necessarily the case. In fact, the play goes out of its way to dramatize Macbeth's deliberation about whether or not he should kill the King. What's more, the three sisters never say anything to Macbeth that is specific about murder. The sisters prophesy that Macbeth will be king, and he comes up with the idea or murder all on his own. So, perhaps the weird sisters don't control Macbeth so much as they are a catalyst. You could argue that they set things in motion and reveal a murderous ambition that's maybe been inside Macbeth all along. There's lots more room for interpretation here so go ahead and take a stab at it.

*Shakespearean tragedies always end in death but with the promise of continuity: Not all tragedies end in death but all of *Shakespeare's* tragedies do. We know things will end badly – we just want to know *how* badly. Macduff, of course, lops off Macbeth's head and then runs and presents it to Malcolm, who will soon be crowned king.

Notice here that, despite the deaths of individuals in the play (King Duncan, the guards, Macduff's wife and kids, Lady Macbeth, the Siward's son, etc.), Shakespeare is also interested in the restoration of political order. Macbeth was kind of a tyrant and made his subjects miserable. Perhaps things will be better with Malcolm on the throne. (Though, there may be a minor hitch, which we talk about in "What's Up With the Ending?")

Macbeth
Shmoop Learning Guide

There's also a strong sense of *England's* own political lineage at work here. Recall, if you will, that in Act IV, Scene i, the weird sisters present a vision of eight kings, all descendents of Banquo. (Banquo was killed by Macbeth's henchman in Act III, Scene iii but his son, Fleance, survived the attack.) King James I of England (a.k.a. King James VI of Scotland), the guy sitting on the throne when Shakespeare wrote *Macbeth*, traced his lineage back to Banquo so, this whole bit gives King James (and England) some props by helping to sustain the Stuart political myth.

So there you have it. *Macbeth* is definitely a tragedy. Is it one of the greatest ever written? We think so (and it's definitely one of the most frightening) but you'll have to read the play and decide that one for yourself.

Tone

Murky, Somber, Sinister, and Foreboding
Literary critics don't call the play Shakespeare's "darkest tragedy" for nothing. It opens with three witches conjuring on a heath amidst thunder, lightening, "fog and filthy air," which establishes a dark and murky atmosphere that permeates *Macbeth* – a play that's full of sinister prophesies, murder, and general wickedness.

Even the humor and seemingly light hearted moments are bleak. In Act II, Scene iii, the Porter famously jokes about who could be knocking at the doors of Macbeth's castle at such an hour. He goes through an extensive comedy routine as he imagines what it would be like to be the porter at the gates of hell. (Pretty busy, apparently, because there's so much evil in the world. Then again, notes the Porter, Macbeth's castle is much too "cold" to be hell.) The joke, of course, is that Macbeth's castle *is* a lot like hell, especially since Macbeth has just murdered Duncan while the king was sleeping. Cue the uncomfortable laughter. Later in the play (act four, scene two) Macduff's young son and his wife crack jokes about how Lady Macduff will have to go to the market to "buy" a new husband, since hers has seemingly abandoned her. And just as we're enjoying a few chuckles, a couple of murderers enter and stab Macduff's son in the guts. So there's that.

Writing Style

Blank Verse in Iambic Pentameter and Prose
Reading any one of Shakespeare's plays can feel like reading a lengthy poem and that's because they're written in a combination of verse (poetry) and prose (how we talk every day). We break all of this down in the paragraphs that follow but here's what you should remember about Shakespeare's plays: The nobility tend to speak in "blank verse," which is a pretty formal way to talk. The commoners or, "Everyday Joes" tend to speak just like we do, in regular old prose. (Note: The play *Richard II* is the *one* exception to this rule – it's the only Shakespeare

Macbeth
Shmoop Learning Guide

play written *entirely* in verse – even the gardeners speak poetry.)

OK. Now, let's think about *Macbeth* specifically.

Blank Verse or, Unrhymed Iambic Pentameter (The Nobles)

In *Macbeth* the noble characters mostly speak in unrhymed "iambic pentameter" (also called "blank verse"). Don't let the fancy names intimidate you – it's simple once you get the hang of it. Let's start with a definition of "Iambic Pentameter:"

An "iamb" is an unaccented syllable followed by an accented one. "Penta" means "five," and "meter" refers to a regular rhythmic pattern. So "iambic pentameter" is a kind of *rhythmic pattern* that consist of *five iambs* per line. It's the most common rhythm in English poetry and sounds like five heartbeats:

ba-DUM, ba-DUM, ba-DUM, ba-DUM, ba-DUM.

Let's try it out on this line, where Lady Macbeth urges her husband to wash his hands after he has murdered King Duncan:

and WASH this FILthy WITness FROM your HAND.

Every second syllable is accented (stressed) so this is classic iambic pentameter. Since the lines have no regular rhyme scheme we call it "Unrhymed Iambic Pentameter," a.k.a. "Blank Verse."

Trochaic Tetrameter with Rhymed Couplets (The Witches)

The witches also speak in verse but it's done in a way that sets them apart from other characters. In fact, they often chant in a sing-song way that sounds a lot like a scary nursery rhyme. Many of their lines are delivered in what's called "trochaic tetrameter" with "rhymed couplets." That's a mouthful but, again, it's actually pretty simple once you wrap your brain around it. Let's take a closer look at "trochaic tetrameter."

A "trochee" is the opposite of an "iamb." It's an accented syllable followed by an unaccented syllable that sounds like DUM-da. "Tetra" means "four" and "meter" refers to a regular rhythmic pattern. So "trochaic tetrameter" is a kind of *rhythmic pattern* that consist of *four trochees* per line. It sounds like this:

DUM-da, DUM-da, DUM-da, DUM-da.

Here's an example from *Macbeth*:

DOUble, DOUble, TOIL and TROUble.
FIre BURN and CAULdron BUbble.

Notice the way the endings of these two lines rhyme (trouble and bubble)? That's what's called a "Rhymed Couplet." (Couplet just means two.) Here's another example:

Macbeth
Shmoop Learning Guide

For a charm of powerful **trouble**,
Like a hell-broth boil and **bubble**.

On the one hand, the meter and the rhyme kind of make the chanting seem a little silly and benign (especially for modern audiences, who don't necessarily believe in witchcraft.). At the same time, however, all the talk about "hell-broth" and "trouble" sounds frightening, especially when what goes into the "hell-broth" consists of disturbing things like "eye of newt" and "finger of birth-strangled babe."

Prose (Commoners)
Not everyone in the play speaks in verse. Ordinary folks, as we've said, don't talk in a special rhythm – they just talk. Check out the Porter's lines:

'Faith sir, we were carousing till the
second cock: and drink, sir, is a great
provoker of three things.
[…]
Marry, sir, nose-painting, sleep, and
urine. Lechery, sir, it provokes, and unprovokes;
it provokes the desire, but it takes
away the performance […]

Notice that it's not just the *type* of speech that sets the Porter apart from the nobles – it's also the *content* of what he says (which is "low" or "common"). Here, the Porter explains that he was up late "carousing" (partying) and then goes on to describe the physical consequences of excessive drinking: a red nose, a frequent urge to urinate, sleepiness, sexual desire, and problems "performing" in bed. The Porter's speech is witty but it's not exactly what you'd call "classy."

What's Up With the Title?
Exactly what you think is up with the title. Shakespeare wasn't a guy to waste words.

That said, we don't want to leave you feeling disappointed so here's a bit of trivia that might interest you. It's considered bad luck to say the play's name out loud—that's why theater folk call it "the Scottish play."

What's Up With the Ending?
We couldn't help it. We just had to take a peek at the ending of the play. Here's what goes down, in case you haven't finished reading the play yet.

Macbeth is slain by Macduff, who lops off Macbeth's head and presents it to Malcolm, the soon to be crowned king. (What? You were expecting something else? This is a Shakespearean tragedy, so it's got to end with a little blood and death, right?)

Macbeth
Shmoop Learning Guide

The thing is, though, Shakespeare's tragedies are also always interested in reestablishing a sense of political order and continuity. So, while Macbeth has been running amok throughout the entire play (killing kings, ordering the murders of children, hanging out with witches, and putting his own selfish needs before the good of the kingdom), we're left with a sense that Malcolm's rule will be a time of healing and restoration…or will it?

After Macbeth's severed head is delivered to the soon-to-be-king, everyone in the vicinity yells out "Hail, King of Scotland" (5.11). Now, where have we heard that before? Oh, we know, that's what the witches call out to Macbeth at the play's beginning, just before all hell breaks loose. You might want to revisit Act I, scene iii, where Macbeth first encounters the weird sisters. We counted, and the witches say "hail" to Macbeth no less than ten times – that word is a loud and creepy echo by the time they're done with it. We can't help but wonder if Malcolm, who is enthusiastically "hailed" as King of Scotland, will be a good ruler or, if he'll turn out to be just as oppressive as Macbeth. This move is pretty typical of Shakespeare. Big Willy *always* likes to leave us guessing.

Did You Know?

Trivia

- In theater circles, *Macbeth* is considered to be an unlucky play. Saying the play's name aloud is considered bad luck – that's why it's often referred to as "the Scottish play."
- At about half the length of Hamlet, Macbeth is one of Shakespeare's shortest plays.
- Some scholars believe that the scenes involving Hecate were added in by later theater writers, not Shakespeare himself. They seemed a good opportunity for the song and dance routines that livened up the otherwise dark play. (Source: Kiefer, Frederick. Shakespeare's Visual Theatre: Staging the Personified Characters. Cambridge, England; New York: Cambridge University Press, 2003. 101.)
- In 1936, the Federal Theater Project sponsored a highly successful version of Macbeth at the Lafayette Theater in Harlem. Featuring an all Black cast and set in post-colonial Haiti, the production was known for spectacular direction and the imposing sounds of drums. It was the first stage production of a young man in his early twenties named Orson Welles. (Source)
- The trio of weird sisters represents a literary convention that was popular in Shakespeare's day: the three Fates as represented by the maiden, the matron, and the hag, or Past, Present, and Future respectively. (Source: Ewing, Thor. Gods and Worshippers in the Viking and Germanic World. Stroud Gloucestershire, England: The History Press Ltd., 2008.)
- Orson Welles's 1948 film of Macbeth was not considered a critical success in the United States. (Source)

Macbeth
Shmoop Learning Guide

Steaminess Rating

PG-13

There are plenty of allusions to sex in *Macbeth* and more times than not, they're about impotence and sterility. The weird sisters cast a spell to "drain" a sailor "dry as hay" so he won't be able to have children with his wife (1.3.4). Lady Macbeth insinuates that her husband is impotent in the bedroom when she goads him into killing King Duncan. In doing so, she also implies that "doing" the deed in the bedroom is like "doing" murder, which prompts Macbeth to declare "I dare *do all* that may become a man" (1.7.3). Macbeth says this, of course, right before he insists that his wife should give birth to male children only so, make of that what you will. (Or, check out "Quotes" for "Gender" if you want to know what *we* think.) Even the Porter's dirty jokes lead to a discussion of male performance (or lack thereof) when he laments that drinking a lot of alcohol puts men in the mood for a little fun but also makes it hard for them to function (2.3.3).

Allusions and Cultural References

Literature, Philosophy, and Mythology

- Tarquin, who raped Lucrece (2.2.55)
- Gorgon or Medusa who turned men to stone (2.3.72)

Historical References

- A farmer: well-known alias for Father Garnet of the Gunpowder Plot (2.2.4)
- The equivocator: central in the Gunpowder Plot against King James I (2.2.8)
- Mark Antony and Caesar (3.1.56)

Best of the Web

Movie or TV Productions

1948 Movie
http://imdb.com/title/tt0040558/
Macbeth, directed by, and starring, Orson Welles, with Jeanette Nolan, Roddy McDowall, and Dan O'Herlihy.

Macbeth
Shmoop Learning Guide

1955 Movie
http://imdb.com/title/tt0048230/
Joe Macbeth, a film noir set in Chicago as a gang war story.

1957 Movie
http://imdb.com/title/tt0050613/
Throne of Blood, a retelling of Macbeth directed by Akira Kurosawa and set in Feudal Japan, starring Toshiro Mifune.

1979 Movie
http://imdb.com/title/tt0079499/
A Performance of Macbeth, 1979 film directed by Trevor Nunn, starring Ian McKellen (a.k.a. Gandalf or Magneto) and Judi Dench.

1991 Movie
http://imdb.com/title/tt0102432/
Men of Respect, a retelling of Macbeth set in New York as a Mafia power struggle and performed in modern English.

1997 Movie
http://imdb.com/title/tt0119591/
Macbeth, a film directed by Jeremy Freeston and Brian Blessed, with Jason Connery as Macbeth and Helen Baxendale as Lady Macbeth.

2001 Movie
http://imdb.com/title/tt0265713/
Scotland, Pa., a modern re-make of Macbeth set in a hamburger stand in 1975 in Pennsylvania.

2003 Movie
http://imdb.com/title/tt0379370/
Maqbool, a Hindi adaptation set in the Mumbai underworld, starring Irfan Khan and Tabu.

2003 Movie
http://imdb.com/title/tt0411618/
Macbeth, an independent film directed by Bryan Enk; set in a surrealistic modern United States. Moira Stone is Lady Macbeth, and Peter B. Brown is Macbeth.

2006 Movie
http://imdb.com/title/tt0434541/
Macbeth, a film directed by Geoffrey Wright and set in Melbourn, Australia amidst gang warfare.

Videos
The Banquet Scene
http://www.youtube.com/watch?v=wu-rE6Nc0QI
The banquet scene from the Royal Shakespeare Company's 1979 production of *Macbeth*,

Macbeth
Shmoop Learning Guide

taped for television, with a young Ian McKellen and a grave Judi Dench masterfully portraying Macbeth and his Lady.

The Banquet Scene
http://www.youtube.com/watch?v=irlPrZ4ulPQ
Watch Macbeth ruin a perfectly good banquet in Polanski's 1971 film.

Orson Welles's Interpretation of Macbeth
http://www.youtube.com/watch?v=QZLrqJka-EU
A news reel clip containing information about Orson Welles's 1936 production of Macbeth for the Federal Theater Project at Harlem's Lafayette Theater. The final scene battle scene is included.

Macbeth, Starring Sock Puppets
http://www.youtube.com/watch?v=Wl0OpUfi26U
A condensed version of the play featuring Scottish sock puppets. Enough said.

This is Macbeth
http://www.youtube.com/watch?v=E4cMHnWIR9k
Check out Flocabulary's "Sound and Fury" Macbeth rap from the Shakespeare is Hip-Hop album. It's educational and surprisingly cool.

Macbeth Rap
http://www.thisismacbeth.com/
A great resource. Dramatic reenactments of the scenes, interviews the characters on a talk show, songs about the plot, and silly commercials that are Macbeth related.

The BBC's *Bitsize* Summary of *Macbeth*
http://www.bbc.co.uk/schools/gcsebitesize/english_literature/dramamacbeth/macbethplotact.shtml
The BBC's hilarious *Bitesize* summary tells the story of Macbeth in under eight minutes.

Reduced Shakespeare Company's *Macbeth*
http://www.youtube.com/watch?v=pQk4Y6Q69u8
Shakespeare meets sketch comedy in this abbreviated performance of the play.

Images

The Text of Macbeth Printed in 1623
http://www.folger.edu/imgdtl.cfm?imageid=731&cid=919
Mr. William Shakespeare's Comedies, Histories, & Tragedies. London: Jaggard, 1623. Opening page of *Macbeth*.

1793 Painting Inspired by Macbeth
http://www.folger.edu/imgdtl.cfm?imageid=100&cid=919
Henry Fuseli. Macbeth consulting the vision of the armed head. Oil on canvas with original inscribed frame, 1793.

Macbeth
Shmoop Learning Guide

The Three Witches
http://www.theatrehistory.com/british/macbeth.jpg
A 1827 painting by Alexandre-Marie Colin.

Documents

Sigmund Freud's Take on the Macbeths
http://web.singnet.com.sg/~yisheng/notes/shakespeare/mbeth_f.htm
This is a psychological analysis that explores the downfall of Lady Macbeth, and the historical context of the Elizabethan transition to James I of Scotland, son of Elizabeth's cousin Mary. Freud highlights the father-son relations in the play, and touches upon the idea of Elizabeth's own childlessness, and the tangle for the throne that ensues, to explain Shakespeare's special treatment of this otherwise well-known story.

"Lady Macbeth, Prickly Pear Queen"
http://books.google.com/books?id=xq4Xbcs6-IAC&pg=PA80&lpg=PA80&dq=lady+macbeth+prickly+pear+queen&source=bl&ots=EDYnkKeyfa&sig=ojG_M-w1pCT1dTQe4vPA-kL1X78&hl=en&ei=yF6dS6fjLIiwsQOp0-C6Ag&sa=X&oi=book_result&ct=result&resnum=6&ved=0CBgQ6AEwBQ#v=onepage&q=lady%20macbeth%20prickly%20pear%20queen&f=false
In Jane Avrich's hilarious short story, Lady Macbeth marries a young fruit mogul (we're not kidding) and baffles everyone with her eccentric behavior. Read it on Google Books.

An Online Copy of Macbeth
http://library.thinkquest.org/2888/
A full text version of the play with links to some definitions and a concise summary following each scene.

The Historical Context of Macbeth
http://homepages.tesco.net/~eandcthomp/macbeth.htm
An interesting article on the historical context of Macbeth with relation to the reign of King James I and then-contemporary law about witchcraft. Shakespeare knew of King James's intense interest in all things supernatural, as he published a tract in 1597 entitled *Daemonologie*, a detailed and scholarly inspection of the subject. Some scholars contend that the scenes of witches and Hecate in the play were included to please the new king.

Printed in Great Britain
by Amazon